SOMETHING'S FISHY

Getting Rid of the Carp in Your Life

SOMETHING'S FISHY

Jay Carty

MULTNOMAH

PORTLAND, OREGON 97266

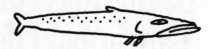

Cover design by Bruce DeRoos
Illustrations by Krieg Barrie
Bubbles by Durand Demlow

SOMETHING'S FISHY
© 1990 by Jay Carty
Published by Multnomah Press
Portland, Oregon 97266

Printed in the United States of America

Multnomah Press is a ministry of Multnomah School of the Bible, 8435 Northeast Glisan Street, Portland, Oregon 97220

<u>Library of Congress Cataloging-in-Publication Data</u>

Carty, Jay.
    Something's fishy : getting rid of the carp in your life / by Jay Carty.
        p.   cm.
    ISBN 0-88070-356-3
    1. Christian life—1960- 2. Carty, Jay. I. Title.
BV4501.2.C3363 1990
248.4—dc20   90-37139
                                                          CIP

90 91 92 93 - 4 3 2 1

CONTENTS

ACKNOWLEDGMENTS

A year-and-a-half ago I had three hundred pages of mishmash I called *Fertilizer for Your Soil*. I thought this book was better than it was. Three publishers said "no way" before I believed them.

But there was one editor who red-lined the volume and made a slug of suggestions to boot. I reworked the manuscript according to her ideas and made another run at it. This time I called it *Something's Fishy* and it was good enough to contract, but not good enough for Liz. So the thing came back to me again for another total rewrite.

In auto racing the tachometer to the red line gets the most out of a car without breaking it. Liz has added a new dimension to the term "red-lining it." She revved me up, took me to my limits, and brought more out than I knew I had—without breaking me. In addition to freely using her red pen, this radiant red-liner had the wisdom to call in the right people to make sure I didn't cause too much trouble, get too far off base, or cause myself too much grief.

If we were in the racing world, Liz would be lovingly called a "red-line momma." It's a compliment that's not genteel enough for use in the dignified world of literature, editors, and books. So I'll just call her Liz. It's a good name. My mother wore it well.

I'll take the flack for the stuff you don't like between the pages. Liz Beth truly gets the credit for the stuff that changes your life.

Once again, Liz Heaney, I'm as grateful as I can be. It was a 'no go' if it weren't for you. Allow me to dedicate the fruit of *Something's Fishy* to our Heavenly Father, but the book is dedicated to you.

You and one other person—if you don't mind.

I don't know him well. Really. We have never had much more than a hello relationship, although I like him more than that. Given the time, there are the makings for a good relationship. Once, I told him how much his message meant to me. But other than that we are brothers in Christ, and not much more.

In the late seventies, Bob was speaking at a Christian Camping International meeting at Mount Hermon Conference Center in California. He spoke of the necessity of keeping the presentation of the Bible's message current with the present culture, without compromising the gospel. That singular message affected me as much as any ever has. So much so, I have shaped my life's work around attempting to do just that.

He didn't know he did it (the instrument often doesn't know when the Master is using him), but Bob Kranning shaped my ministry before *Yes! Ministries* was ever born. And *Something's Fishy* is an attempt at speaking to a huge portion of our population that would never read *Something's Stuffy*.

You're to blame, Bob. So, along with Liz Heaney, I dedicate this book to you with gratitude and thanks.

Special Thanks

I offer special thanks to you Paul Westphall, Neal Arnold, Lou Shelton, and Marvin DeGroff for proof-reading a manuscript; to Jack and Melanie Glubrecht for minding the store while I wrote; to Mary, my wife, for letting me take the time; and to Ernie Johnson for all the fish stories.

DEFINITIONS

Carp
A fish.
A non-Christian.
Sin that renders the believer powerless, which keeps a nonbeliever from believing.

Bass
A fish.
A sold-out, on-fire, goin'-for-it, Jesus-lovin' believer.

Trout
A fish.
A lukewarm Christian who may or may not be saved. Most people assume trout are saved, but they are either carp or bass dressed to look like trout.

A carp in trout's clothing
A non-Christian who is thought to be a believer.

A bass in trout's clothing
A believer who has allowed a little carp back into his or her life and has become lukewarm.

Tweener

Same as trout. Someone in between. Can't tell if he or she is or isn't. Only God knows.

"Christian"

Same as trout and tweener.

Christian

Bass. No carp. Can be a bass dressed as a trout.

Iffy

Same as tweener. Same as lukewarm. Same as trout. Maybe saved, maybe not. Who knows? Only God.

Luke

Short for lukewarm. A bass dressed like a trout.

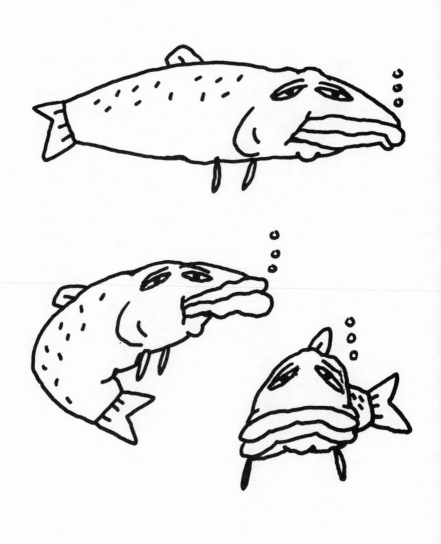

THE STORY OF THE THREE UGLY TROUTLINGS

I'm sure you remember the story of the ugly duckling. It was a tale about a little guy who was being raised by ducks. He thought he was a duck and everybody else thought he was a duck, too. But he didn't look like a duck and he couldn't do the things ducks did. He couldn't because he wasn't a duck. He was a swan. But he had to grow up before everyone realized that.

There is an age-old, seldom-told story about three ugly troutlings that is similar to the ugly duckling story. As the tale was told to me, these three little trout were raised in separate ponds. For the sake of time I'll summarize.

The carp ate the first ugly troutling.

The second ugly troutling discovered he was a bass. As soon as he realized it, he ate the carp.

The third ugly troutling was a carp. But the bass thought he was a trout and didn't eat him. Since the bass thought this, the carp thought he was a trout, too. So the other fish let the carp they thought was a trout live in the pond. He grew up, got married, and had lots of little carp who were raised to think they were trout.

There were then so many trout that quite a few of the bass wished they could be trout, and began dressing like them. Now there are so many carp who think they are trout, and so many bass who look like trout, the bass are being squeezed out of the pond. That's what happens when you let a little carp into your pond.

One day the sky that Chicken Little thought was falling actually did. All the fish in the third pond were killed.

Carp do not go to fish heaven, but bass do. None of the carp who thought they were trout went. And there weren't many bass left to go.

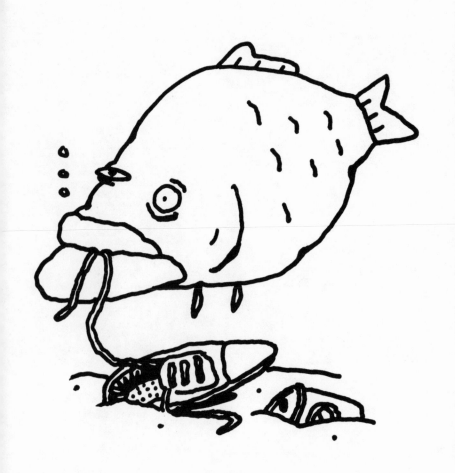

CARP

Carp are bottom fish. As they cruise the murky waters, their ugly lips turn downward and play vacuum cleaner, sucking up the stuff that settles. They're scavengers. I think of them as scumsuckers. They especially like fish eggs.

Like rats and mice, carp are prolific breeders. And they are hardy—they can survive wide swings in temperature. The critters are hard to kill, too. Large, thick, armorlike scales protect their sides, and their rib cage goes all the way around their body, providing unusual protection. Those suckers are bony and tough.

In some countries carp are considered a delicacy. But not in the good old U.S. of A. Carp are a trash fish here. I understand why.

My friend Ernie told me about how he and his buddy would go to the slaughterhouse, scoop up handfuls of coagulated blood, and walk back to the Columbia Slough. Environmental controls were unheard of in those days, so there was a drainage ditch from the slaughter house to the slough. Blood and guts flowed openly and unchecked. Where the ditch ended and the slough began was the residence of thousands of carp. Some up to forty pounds . . . just cruisin' in and consumin' all that yuck.

Ernie would moosh some blood clots on a hook and heave it into those ugly waters. Bingo! He caught a fish every time. They loved it. But he only caught carp. Nothing else was there.

It was the same at the dam. Not all fish make it to the fish ladder. Some go through the turbines. That makes for a lot of chum on the other side. Well, guess what's forty feet long, thirty feet deep, and fifteen feet thick. A wall of carp—feeding on fish guts and parts coming through the turbine exhaust.

Some years ago, a logging company introduced some large goldfishlike carp to a dirty log pond. They thought the carp would clean the lake. They were wrong. In fact, there was a dramatic decline in the brown trout population of the pond. When a heavy rain washed some of the golden boys over the dam, it only took a few months before the local fishermen noticed a rapid demise in the trout population downstream. The carp had taken over. The problem was solved when they introduced bass into the pond and river. Bass beat carp every time . . . they eat the carp fry and so are an effective way to control the carp population.

The moral of the story? When you harbor carp, they quickly take over and drive out the good fish. Carp breed carp.

Most lakes and large rivers contain lots of different fish. But have you noticed, the fewer the carp, the better the fishin'? Conversely, the more carp there are, the worse the fishin' will be.

There is something fishy in Christendom and I know what it is: *Carp.* Now I'm not talkin' fish here, I'm talking sin . . . deception. I'm talkin' bout people who think they are Christians but aren't. Let me explain.

People call themselves Christians but instead are spawning grounds for carp (sin). In some churches a permissive philosophy is being preached that makes it okay to cultivate the critters. Having a little carp in a life just isn't considered that big of a deal. "I've killed the big ones, and that's good enough," is the attitude of some. Others don't even worry about the big ones. They live life just as they please.

But carp take over . . . they will eat your fry, root you out of church, and mess up your home.

Part of what I'd like to accomplish in this book is to help you get rid of the carp in your life by becoming an aggressive, "kick carp" bass who's sold out to Christ. We'll look at what it takes to become a bass.

But first, we're going to go on a carp hunt and deal with a very important question: How much carp can be in a life and still have that life be considered a good fishin' hole? Or, how bad can I be and still get into the kingdom of God? Can a Christian live like a non-Christian and really be saved?

A lot of people are asking those questions today. Hopefully, by the time you finish this book you will decide for yourself: Which am I?

Am I a carp?

or

Am I a Jesus-lovin,' "kick carp" bass?

If you're neither of these, perhaps you'd call yourself a trout. But remember, trout are either carp or bass dressed in trout's clothes. Trout need to wrestle with an important question: Has God drawn lines in the midst of fuzzy gray? Can a fish dressed in trout's clothing really go to heaven?

Trout who refuse to deal with the carp in their lives may be revealing the true nature of their heart.

Carp are a big deal to God. People whose lives are full of carp are middle-of-the-roaders—in this book I've coined several phrases for people the Bible calls lukewarm: trout, tweeners, iffy, luke . . . "Christian" (notice the quotation marks). You can't tell if they are really Christian or not. They live in the middle. Some are, some aren't. Only God knows for sure. If that's you, I hope this book gets your attention.

God got my attention in 1970. That's when he initiated the hunt for carp in my life. I didn't have to look very long. I definitely had a school of 'em swimmin'. I'll tell you what happened in the next chapter.

1

CARP IN MY LIFE

I was twenty-nine years old and had been in the "secret service" for fifteen years. (I prayed to receive Christ when I was fourteen.) You couldn't tell by the way I acted, and you couldn't tell by my speech. There wasn't much evidence of the Lord in my life during those years.

After we married, Mary and I started attending church again. On our third Sunday a guy came up to me and said, "There's a couples' conference at a Christian retreat center in a few weeks. I don't know if you've ever been to one, but my wife and I are planning on going and we'd like you to go, too. It will make your wife happy and we'll have plenty of time to become friends. I'd like to be your friend. It only costs fifteen bucks for your deposit. Surely, a friendship is worth fifteen dollars. What do you think?"

It was pure manipulation. What was I going to say, "Naw, your friendship's not worth fifteen bucks"?

So I coughed up the dough. However, two days

before the conference my friend couldn't go. My reason for going had gone, but I had fifteen nonrefundable bucks invested, and I'm pretty tight with a dollar, so we went.

It was a long drive, and we got there late. Dinner was cold. Before they'd even let me eat, they made me fork out another forty-five bucks. I don't know what I expected, but sixty bucks for a weekend in the early 1970s at a Christian conference center seemed like a lot of money. Hume Lake was in the boonies in the mountains east of Fresno; there was no other place to go. I was stuck, so I grudgingly handed over the money.

I don't know what I thought the weekend would be like. I never dreamed I'd end up in church, but that's where you go on Friday night at a Christian conference center. They called it a meeting, but they couldn't fool me. I was in church.

I thought to myself, *Well, at least I'll go fishing at the lake in the morning*. But after breakfast on Saturday do you know where I was? That's right, church . . . the morning meeting.

Quite frankly, that ruined my afternoon. And after dinner you know where I was by now . . . that place again . . . meetin'. We did it twice more on Sunday. I couldn't believe it! I'd paid sixty bucks to go to church on Friday night, Saturday morning, Saturday night, and twice on Sunday. I could have stayed home and gone once for nothing.

On Saturday night, the speaker, Ken Poure, had been talking about husband and wife stuff. As good as he was I could hardly wait to get out of there. I was moving from cheek to cheek, just like you do on Sunday mornings in church. As he finished he said, "We're going to pray."

I said to myself, "Super, in about fifteen seconds we can jet."

There were just two kinds of prayer for me in those days. First, if you were in deep dark serious trouble you threw one up and hoped it didn't come down. How long does that take? Certainly not more than five or ten seconds. The other kind might be something you'd do before you ate. Someone used to say, "Hey, aren't you going to talk to your plate?" I'd say, "Sure. Hey plate, let's eat."

That was prayer for me and it didn't take long at all. I'm not being blasphemous. That's the way it was. So I figured when this guy said we're going to pray, it would take less than a minute and we would be out of there.

Five minutes went by. Listen, five minutes is an eternity when you're expecting less than a minute. Since there was no sign of a letup I started daydreaming, like you do on Sunday mornings sometimes.

I tuned back in about fifteen minutes later. They were still praying. There were a hundred and twenty people in the room—sixty couples—and a man stood up. I knew he was standing because I was peekin' during prayer. I figured that one guy peeking wouldn't invalidate the whole thing.

The man standing prayed, "God would you forgive me? I haven't been a spiritual leader for my family." He then touched his wife on the shoulder. As she looked up, there were tears running down her face as he continued, "Honey, would you forgive me, and would you help me to become the kind of man God wants me to be?" I heard somebody sniff.

I was thinking, *Let me out of here.*

Then a woman stood. I knew she was standing because I was peeking. Tears were coming down her face

27

as she prayed, "God, I've been so dominant in my household spiritually. Forgive me." She touched her husband, waited for their eyes to meet, and continued praying between sobs. "Would you forgive me, and would you help me to become the kind of woman God wants me to be?"

I thought a rash of hay fever had hit the place.

Everybody started sniffing and blowing their noses. People were crying.

These people are all freaks and weirdoes. Let me out of here!

That's when my wife stood up.

I could have killed her! I knew everyone would expect me to pray next. Everyone knew the big guy . . . the ex-Laker. If I didn't pray next, think how much face I'd lose. If I did, think how much more face I'd lose. I didn't know how to do it. And being your classic competitive jock I figured I had been challenged to a pray-off.

Sitting there, I got through my anger and heard what she prayed. My heart jumped into my throat and beat loudly. *Ka Kunk, ka kunk* echoed in my head. My palms got real sweaty.

Ken Poure (remember, he was the one leading the meeting.) said, "We can't stop yet. I'm absolutely convinced there's someone sitting out there whose heart is beating up in their throat." He really said that; I'm not kidding. He also said, "And your palms are probably real sweaty right now."

I was unconsciously wiping my palms off on my pants thinking, *It's not me, oh no, it's not me.*

He said, "That's the Spirit of God tugging on you. Let go. Let him have you. Give up!"

I was mad because I thought Poure had been peeking

during prayer.

It took a few moments of soul searching and letting God work, but I finally stood up. Our heavenly Father was starting to clean the carp out of my life. I was crying. Tears come easily to me. (A good TV commercial will make me cry, but it's got to be a good one.) However, this wasn't just tears or sobs, I was convulsive. It was embarrassing, but I prayed.

I'm so glad God looks on the heart and not our words, because eloquent I was not. I said, "God, I don't fully understand everything that's going on right now, but I acknowledge that you made me, therefore you must know what's best for me. I have now proven that I don't. So, I want to take my hands off my life and give control over to you. I don't know what that will mean, but I don't want to run it anymore. I don't want to say no to you anymore. I know I will say it, but in my heart I don't want to. If you can still use me, I'm yours." I sat down. That was it. It was now open season on Carty's carp.

Things moved swiftly after that. He put a 'Paul' named Sam in my life who became my discipler. I remain his 'Timothy'. Mary and I worked with college people at our church. A few years later we directed a Christian conference center. I assumed a role as the Northwest Director for Churches Alive five years after that, and started Yes Ministries in late 1981. Our desire was to help people say "Yes!" to God.

We thought about naming our organization Perhaps Ministries or Occasionally Ministries, or When I Feel Like It Ministries. But that's just carp. We went with "Yes!" And that says it all.

If you had told me twenty years ago I'd be doing what I'm doing today, I would have laughed in your face. There are people I run into now who remember my foul mouth and say, "You're a what?" God works in mysterious ways.

People occasionally ask if I have a life verse. Being 6' 8" tall, I usually say Isaiah 28:20 ("The bed is too short to stretch out on, the blanket too narrow to wrap around you."). But that's just for fun. My real life verse has become:

> Search me, O God, and know my heart; test me and know my anxious thoughts. See if there is any offensive way in me, and lead me in the way everlasting" (Psalm 139:23, 24).

Would you like God to do that with you? It's a carp-removing verse for those who will pray it vigorously and often. Do that now before going any further.

I'm serious, if you read this sentence before praying, stop reading and pray through the verse before continuing. Don't start our time together being naughty.

Now for the big question: *When did I become a Christian?*

As I look back on that fifteen-year period between praying to receive Christ at fourteen and selling out at twenty-nine, it's clear my faith wasn't evident. I was a trout who lived in Tweener's Bog, the area that's in between unbelief and all-out commitment. My life was typified by "carpola," and lots of 'em.

Although I hadn't come right out and said it, I guess I was asking *How bad can I be and still get into heaven?* No . . . *How good do I have to be to just barely get in.*

Understand that I wasn't bad as some people would define bad. But neither was I good as some would define good. I was satisfied in the lagoon of lukewarm, in the flow and flux of the fuzzy gray. Just like Luke Warren Trout. You'll read about him in the next chapter.

As we start our hunt, ask yourself:

How much carp is in my life? Is it enough to make you wonder about your relationship with God?

2

WHAT ABOUT LUKE WARREN TROUT?

It was another typical day at the Sand Bar. The guys had come as a school to enjoy the currents and down a few wet ones. Luke was there, too. He'd been coming more often recently.

The Sand Bar was a club on the edge of Backslider's Basin. Actually, no one was sure if it was in B.S. Basin or Tweener's Bog. The fellows had been arguing over that for years. But no one around these parts really cared. The only time it came up was when someone got religion and headed for Kick Carp Lake. Although that happened to Bob Bass, it didn't happen very often.

Carp came to the Sand Bar from Backslider's Basin and Tweener's Bog. The place could get real rough sometimes. Those Backslider's guys were pretty tough. But there were always a few trout from the bog hanging around. That usually calmed things a bit. Sometimes there were a lot of trout, and when that happened, quite frankly, it was hard to tell the trout from the carp.

Luke Warren Trout had been a resident of Tweener's

Bog for some years now. Luke had been on the edge of Kick Carp Lake. He may have even gone in once, but he wasn't sure. He got real close though. He remembers when very clearly.

Luke's brush with Kick Carp Lake was with a bunch of bass, right after he went to that couples' conference with Tillie's church. His wife had so wanted him to go. Actually, she had made the reservations and sprung the trip on him as a surprise. He went to make her happy.

It was the last night of the conference. Luke felt he should go forward with some of the other fish folk. The preacher leading the meeting termed it an altar call. As he looks back on that evening, Luke remembers all the bass. Especially Bob. They had all gone as carp, but they left as bass. Interesting! And then there was the excitement of heading to Kick Carp Lake. Ol' Bob led the pack. That wasn't exciting for Luke. He wasn't all that interested in going. The Bog had been his home for years and he liked it there.

He had put on some trout's clothing that night, which seemed to make Tillie very happy, but he had never followed the rest of the school all the way into Kick Carp Lake. He hadn't even looked under his trout clothes to see what kind of fish he really was. Luke seemed satisfied looking like a trout. Why not? Everyone else seemed pleased. "At least he's not a carp" is what the folks at church said.

Luke liked the fish eggs in the bowls on the bar. *Ummmmmm, better than popcorn.* And he was starting to think about the pickled worms a little earlier each day, along with the chum that chased them down. *It was something to look forward to.* He soothed himself with another swig.

His Chum Light tasted good, and after three he

started to mellow out. Luke grew melancholy and took a look around the room.

"Hi Carl! How's it goin'?" He waved a fin.

Carl Carp was a real playfish and he made no bones about it. He was a carp, knew it, and flaunted it. Always kept a few ladies on the line, stringing them along. *Lucky dogfish, he's got it made*. Carl had only one fin to wave. Karla Carp had a hold on the other. They were leaving for Carl's place.

I should go home. Tillie will be worried again, Luke told himself. She seemed to be worried more and more of the time. But it wasn't long until Luke's thoughts wandered from Tillie to Teresa, the barfish.

Teresa Trout had seemed interested in Luke's story about church and going forward at a meeting. It became a topic of conversation last week when Luke stopped by the Sand Bar on his way home. Some TV evangelist had come on after a ball game had ended. Nobody had changed the channel. That's how they got on the subject. She had gone forward too, years ago. Luke and Teresa talked about it as she passed out Chum Lights to the guys.

After a few more chums, Teresa was lookin' pretty good to Luke. He had forgotten all about Tillie. And after exchanging a few more glances he decided to say yes to her invitation for another chum at her place.

As Teresa took off her clothes, Luke noticed her scales. She was a carp after all. He turned out the light as he took off his. He didn't want to know what he really was. Right now, well, he just didn't care.

>●< >●< >●<

Is there anything sneakier than sin? If so, I don't know what. It starts subtly and builds. Sin is like water that freezes in a crevice of a rock, breaking off a huge hunk. A blade of grass poking through an asphalt pathway. The ant that finds the spilled syrup and goes off to gather his friends. Sin divides, destroys, and builds on itself. But it starts out small. Usually with just a bite. That's the way it was for Eve. Then it grows and spreads like a cancer.

Deception is sin's forerunner. We've all been deceived at some time in our life.[1] It even happened to Paul.[2] He had the nerve to warn us two times, "Do not be deceived."[3] Isn't that a bit like the pot calling the kettle black? Yeah, but since we're all sinners, I guess it's okay. Maybe if we all warned each other a lot, we wouldn't be deceived as often. That's what *Something's Fishy* is all about. Me, a sinner warning you, a sinner.

Reason and rationalization are deception's friends. We are very capable of kidding ourselves. But we can't kid God. He will not be mocked.[4] You can't put one over on him.[5] So we shouldn't waste our time trying. But we do. We've all justified our sin to ourselves at one time or another.

Are you like Luke Warren Trout? Is your life typified by worldliness? Perhaps you can see yourself in the following attitudes:

> "Sure, I'm religious, I just want to keep my life in balance," are the words of the man who refuses to get excited about the Lord who died to save him. He wants his work and play more than his faith.

"Some people get so fanatical about religion. My dad was that way. Well, not this girl!" were the remarks of a woman on her way to her daily aerobics class. She had been raised in a Christian home and was a pastor's kid. She's a fanatic about her health, but not about the Lord.

"I'm looking forward to financial security and an early retirement so I can give back to society some of what has been given to me," are the words of a double-minded businessman. It's easy to let the development of your financial portfolio get in the way of your faith.

"I love driving my BMW. I love working out. I love making money. I love my new house. Oh, and I love God too." It's hard to get saved when you don't love the Lord more than the things in this life.

Do you value things, money, and/or goals more than you value Christ? Embracing the world's values will result in a lot of carp and can even keep you out of heaven. Watch out!

> *If you don't have a desire to please the Father, your spiritual state is a big question mark.*

Jesus made a frightening statement at the end of his Sermon on the Mount.

Not everyone who says to me, "Lord, Lord," will enter the kingdom of heaven, but only he who does the will of my Father who is in heaven.

Many will say to me on that day, "Lord, Lord, did we not prophesy in your name, and in your name drive out demons and perform many miracles?" Then I will tell them plainly, "I never knew you. Away from me, you evil-doers!" (Matthew 7:21-23)

These were people who identified with Christ! They used his name . . . as do "Christians" today.

Jesus is warning the true church to watch out for fakes.

The word *many* in the passage means "much." Some consider it to mean almost a majority. And it didn't just refer to the casual, panhandler passerby who stopped in for the Macfishwich luncheon special that may have been served on the hillside that day. No siree bob! He referred to all the folks who called him Lord. *Therefore, Jesus confirmed: There are a lot of people who call themselves "Christian" who won't be in the kingdom.*

What a scary thought! Can it really be true? Jesus thought so. I'll bet what Jesus said scared the hell right out of some of them by scaring some right into the kingdom. Let me pause to ask a question:

Is there any reason for you to wonder if you might hear the words, "I never knew you. Away from me, you evildoer"? What does your life reflect?

Yes, the Bible does say it's possible to go to church on Sunday and act like hell the rest of the week—and still be a Christian. Paul wrote to the church of Corinth and called them worldly:

Brothers, I could not address you as spiritual but as worldly—mere infants in Christ (1 Corinthians 3:1).

The word he used meant "having the nature of flesh, sensual, controlled by animal appetites, governed by human nature instead of by the Spirit of God."[6] Paul calls them Christians—and he didn't use quotation marks, either.

Lot was like the Corinthians. He wore trout's clothes, too. His greed showed when he chose to go to Las Vegas (Sodom). And he didn't want to leave, even when told by an angel that God was going to snuff the place in the morning. He liked it so much he even chose to make his departure time a close call. After all, he was known in the gates . . . the gates of the gay district.[7] He wanted all the gusto he could get, and it cost him his wife. She wanted to stay so badly she took one last peek and added a new dimension to the term, "She's a salty ol' gal." Lot got so drunk his own daughters raped him. Talk about a lot of carp in your life. But contrary to Judas, Lot believed just enough to sneak into the kingdom.[8] He is one of those rare examples of a bass dressed in trout's clothing.

Lot made it to heaven—by the skin of his teeth. Lot was one lucky dude . . . but people like him are the exception rather than the rule. John wrote the following about certain pewsitters in his church:

> Dear children, this is the last hour; and as you have heard that the antichrist is coming, even now many antichrists have come. This is how we know it is the last hour. They went out from us, but *they did not really belong to us*. For if they had belonged to us, they would have remained with us; but their going showed that none of them belonged to us (1 John 2:18-19, italics mine).

Carp were in the church—dressed as trout—and John didn't know it!

There have been some big name trout in the church. Judas is one. He dressed like a trout while he hung out with Jesus. For three years! But he caved in . . . for some silver. Pilfering funds from the treasury and accepting a contract for a set-up on Christ. It's difficult to believe that anyone could be that close to Jesus and remain a carp. I guess it happens when hearts stay hard.

Be honest, now. Does this describe your life in Christ? Are you lukewarm? Are you a trout? Don't lie to yourself—and don't read on until you have decided.

(I am writing this as filler to trap you, just like I did before. Most people disregard directions. You probably kept on reading and ignored my question. If you're being naughty, stop right here and don't read until you've decided.)

"I'LL SPIT YOU OUT OF MY MOUTH!"

Back in my college days we couldn't drink water during basketball practice. Something about being tough. I'd lose eight to ten pounds during a three-hour period. Once I actually lost fourteen. We've since learned how drinking liquids improves performance. When I work out these days, I usually lose three to five pounds of water, even though I'm drinking. It would be nice if I could lose fat that easily, but I drink the weight back by the next day. Both then and now, when the workout is completed, there is only one thing on my mind. A cold drink. My body wants liquid and I crave cold.

If I'm at the athletic club, I'll choose the fruit punch with all the salts to reestablish my body's chemistry balance. If I'm practicing with the Corvallis High School basketball team, it's a trip to 7/11 for a 44-ounce magnum of Diet Pepsi.

Usually I'm frugal. I want my money's worth. But when I'm real thirsty, strangely enough, my concern is for cold, not quantity. That's why I load up with ice. And I drink it as fast as I can. The goal is to stay as close to having an ice cream headache as I can without actually getting one (few things in life hurt as much).

That first blast of carbonation is heaven, but it's got to be cold. At a time like that, when my body is insisting on icy, there is nothing worse than a drink that's room temperature.

Gag! Yuck! I hate lukewarm. It makes me want to wretch.

Oregon gets some cold spells during the winter. And there is always a lot of rain. Since I travel a lot when there's some work to be done outside around the house, I have to do it when I'm home regardless of the weather. Sometimes it's nasty. Working in inclement weather isn't so bad as long as there is a warm fire to cozy up to and a hot drink waiting. But it's got to be hot. At times like that, I want to warm my hands on the cup and feel the steam rising in my face. Coming in from the cold and being greeted by lukewarm is a letdown of the worst kind.

Every first-aid person knows that if a person consumes something poisonous, and vomiting is called for, nothing is better than lukewarm dishwater. Hot won't do it. Neither will cold. But lukewarm will do the trick every time. Lukewarm will make you call the Irishman . . . OOOROURRRRKE!!!

Christ was at the right hand of God the Father when he instructed John to write seven letters to seven churches. The note to the church at Laodicea deserves our attention:

41

> I know your deeds, that you are neither cold nor hot. I wish you were either one or the other! So, because you are lukewarm—neither hot nor cold—I am about to spit you out of my mouth (Revelation 3:15, 16).

These people were spiritually lukewarm and they made Jesus puke. I know, he used the term "spit you out of my mouth," but it best translates as barf. Lukewarm "Christians" are enough to gag a maggot, is what Christ is saying.

Lukewarm means insincere, dead, and indifferent. Hot is what we're looking for. Goin'-for-it believers. Those who are cold spiritually are easier to deal with than those who are in the no-man's-land of lukewarm. You can talk to the unsaved about Christ because they are upfront about where they are spiritually. But tweeners are something else. Who knows where they are? What's underneath the facade? Who knows?

I speak in a lot of churches, and when I ask audiences where they would place themselves spiritually, most (80 percent) admit they aren't sold out for Christ. That concerns me. No—that *scares* me. Because, if you're not sold-out, then I figure you must be unsaved or in the fuzzy gray of lukewarm. And I believe most lukewarm "Christians" aren't Christian. I hope I'm wrong. I'm glad I'm not the one to make that call. There are lots of referees in the stands, it's the one on the floor who can foul you out. God is the one in stripes.

Faith in saying "the prayer" may have saved Luke Warren Trout, but faith in a prayer doesn't consitute saving faith. So, Luke may be content professing to be what he isn't. Luke Warren Trout certainly isn't on fire for Jesus. On that we can agree. But he's not entirely cold to the things of God either. Luke Warren is . . . well . . . lukewarm. His behavior suggests need for concern—as does the behavior of anyone who fits the description of a tweener.

><><><

Tillie Warren had just finished reading a bedtime story about lukewarm trout to her little girl Bonnie. The mother preferred having her husband there to share these moments, but Luke hadn't come home yet. She didn't know where he was again.

"Are all lukewarm 'Christians' unsaved?" was Bonnie's question when they finished.

"No, not all."

"Most?"

"Probably."

"Are most 'Christians' lukewarm?"

"That's a hard question honey. Sometimes it seems that way."

"Mommy, do you think Daddy is lukewarm?"

Tillie answered her daughter's question without words. A tear fell and she turned, hoping Bonnie wouldn't see.

WRAP UP

1. People who sin without a struggle are probably not saved.
2. Most lukewarm "Christians" are not saved.

3

NEVER TRUST A FISH

I had been speaking at a high school raft rally on the Deschutes River in Oregon. Can you imagine 260 young people in two-man rafts with four or five people in each, shooting the rapids? It was quite a sight.

One evening a girl (I'll call her Nancy) approached me and wanted to chat. I had just finished a sex talk entitled "Sometimes It's Sin and Sometimes It's Not, or, Will I Burn If I Get the Hots?" She had a sexy look about her, the kind a young man on the prowl would be attracted to. Her opening statement was, "My boyfriend and I do everything there is to do, except have intercourse. Therefore, we don't think we're sinning. What do you think?"

I cut through the smoke screen when I asked, "Nancy, do you know Jesus personally?"

Caught off guard she responded belligerently, "I've prayed the prayer." Her look and body language spoke much more. It was as if she were saying, "Naa naa naa naa naa, I can do anything I want to because I prayed the prayer."

My next words were spoken lovingly but firmly. "Nancy, you may be saved. I don't know. My job is to judge your behavior, not you. God will do that. But do you think people who ask 'How bad can I be and still get into the kingdom' are in?"

She paused and thought. "Some," was her quiet, somewhat subdued, response.

"I agree with you. I think some might be saved, too. Are you one of them?"

She went back to her original question and was getting upset, "Do you think we are sinning?"

"Yes, and because of your attitude I doubt your salvation, too. I don't sense a heart for God. Nancy, I'd like to spend some time with you and talk about it."

"Well, that's your opinion," she said as she stomped off. The conversation was over and we never made eye contact again.

A classic tweener. Was Nancy saved? Maybe, but I doubt it. Judging by her response, so does she.

Nancy wasn't committed to Christ and she didn't see herself as a sinner. Her heart was the same as it had always been. Hard!

People like Nancy dream up strange criteria for evaluating their condition before God. Nancy's was "I prayed the prayer didn't I?"

Another criterion people have is goodness; they believe bad people go to hell and good people go to heaven. They see life like golf on a three-par course. They assume that those who get on the green in one shot are good enough for heaven, because only good golfers can do that. Those who hit into the rough or the traps are bound for hell. Terrible golfers are easy to spot, just like rotten people. However, it's hard to tell about the players who take two strokes to get to the green and then two-putt to get in the hole. And who knows about those who one-putt to get their par? Surely they must be okay . . .

It's fuzzy, isn't it?

In golf I know how good is. The pros are good. And guys who shoot par are good. But how good is pretty good? How good is good enough? And what about all the occasionally-playing duffers who vastly outnumber the good players? Well, the scale varies according to who you are talking to, how old they are, how long they've been playing, and who their standard is. That's why man's standards are so variable and wishy-washy.

In life, I know how good good is. God has given us a standard. Christ is good. All the rest of us are duffers.

It's true that life can be equated to golf, except this is competition. You have to get a hole-in-one to get into heaven. Only there's one catch, this isn't a par three you're playing, it's a one-par and *the hole is five hundred yards long.* You can't even make a hole-in-one by accident, because no one can drive a ball that far in one shot. Except for Jesus, that is. Not only can he drive the green in one, he has never hit anything but a hole-in-one. And he'll play for you if you ask him to.

It's impossible to be good enough to go to heaven. And like Nancy, who thought she could say a prayer and be in the kingdom, those who think they can get there on good behavior will miss the boat.

There are a plethora (I've always loved that word!) of beliefs that give people false assurance of their salvation. As we evaluate the reality of our relationship with God, not only should we be careful about what we listen to, it's equally important to evaluate who's saying it. We want to make sure we place our trust in credible sources.

I'm not advocating becoming a skeptic—there are times to trust. And being a little naive is refreshing at times. But when it comes down to your personal relationship with God, it's dangerous to seek the assurance of salvation from others. Heaven and hell are on line.

DON'T TRUST THE EXPERTS

A few years ago a friend read a letter in church one Sunday morning as a prologue to the pastor's sermon. It's a good reminder that the experts aren't always right. Sometimes they are full of carp.

To: Jesus, son of Joseph,
      Woodcrafters Carpenter Shop
      Nazareth

From: Jordan Management Consultants
      Jerusalem

Dear Sir,

Thank you for submitting the resumes of the twelve men that you've picked for management positions in your new organization. All of them have now taken our battery of tests and we've run the results through our computer and have given them personal interviews with our psychologist and vocational aptitude consultants. Here are the conclusions.

It's the staff opinion that most of your nominees are lacking in background, education, and vocational aptitude for the type of enterprise that you're undertaking. They do not have the team concept. We would recommend you continue your search for persons with experience in managerial ability and proven capability.

Simon Peter is emotionally unstable, given to fits of temper. Andrew has absolutely no qualities of leadership. The two brothers, James and John, the sons of Zebedee, place personal interest above company loyalty. Thomas demonstrates a questioning attitude that would tend to undermine morale. We feel that it's our duty to tell you that Matthew has been blacklisted by the Greater Jerusalem Better Business Bureau. James, the son of Alphaeus, and Thaddaeus, definitely have radical leanings. Both registered a high score on the manic-depressive scale.

One of the candidates however shows great potential. He's a man of ability and resourcefulness. He meets people well, has a keen business mind, and has contacts in high places. Is highly motivated, ambitious, responsible. We recommend Judas Iscariot as your controller, treasurer, and righthand man.

All the other profiles are self-explanatory. We wish you every success in your adventure.

Sincerely yours,

The Jordan Management Consultants[1]

It's a good thing Jesus didn't take their advice. But then he knew you can't trust the experts.

The apostle Paul told the people at Berea what to do. At the time there wasn't a bigger shot in the land. Paul was numero uno. But the people at Berea didn't just jump at what he said. Instead, they read their Bibles to see if what Paul said was true. The Bereans always checked out any supposed truths they heard against the

Word of God to make sure truth is what they had heard.

In this day and age we'd better not trust the experts. There are a lot of wolves with good intentions walking around in sheep's clothing saying that if a person has had some experience, he or she is saved. There are professors and pastors who are taking sides and arguing whether or not praying a sinner's prayer solves the problem of salvation. Regardless of the experts' intentions or theology, there is no way they can know a person's heart. It is ever so dangerous to pronounce another person saved.

> *Don't let any expert interpret your emotion, reaction, condition, or experience and convince you of your salvation. They do not know your heart.*

WARNING!! If you have been given a false assurance of your salvation, you are still lost in sin. And you are more difficult to save now than before because you think you are already born again.

DON'T TRUST YOUR PEERS

My dad had a Ford/Mercury agency when I was in high school and college. After graduation it was time to see if I wanted to be involved in the family business.

I was twenty-one and newly married. By that time Dad had acquired a partner, and the partner's father was a salesman at the dealership. When I came on as a salesman, the agency had a problem with double nepotism. Two dad and son combinations. We had the makin's for big trouble.

I was a natural salesman, but was green as grass. The rest of the sales staff initiated me by taking advantage of my ignorance and naiveté, especially Charlie, my dad's partner's father.

There is a term in the car business called "split." It's what happens when someone helps you close a deal. The result is that you split the commission. The big question was, "What constitutes a split?" A ruling was always decreed by the house, and the house was presided over by my father.

I had gone along with several seemingly unfair splits assuming that when the tables were turned I'd get a break. It didn't take long to realize my dad would always rule against me. He didn't want to give anyone grounds for accusing him of playing favorites. The other salesmen quickly realized what was happening and descended on me like ravenous wolves on a defenseless baby fawn. Especially Charlie.

I had to do something about the situation. I formulated a marvelously sneaky plan.

I knew if I made Charlie mad he would cuss me out and leave the dealership until he cooled down. I counted on that when he approached me demanding a split he didn't have coming. I knew what would send him over the edge, used it against him, and the results went just as planned.

Well, the carp hit the fan, and I was called into the office. My dad, his partner, and the head salesman were all there. This was what I was waiting for. It was show time.

They asked me to tell my story, so I did, with the utmost accuracy . . . except I reversed the roles. I put Charlie in my place and me in Charlie's.

Without consulting his partner or the head salesman, my dad made the ruling. "Charlie gets the whole commission. That's it. I don't want to hear anymore about it."

"That's not fair," I bellowed, faking frustration as best I could. My dad had just ruled in my favor thinking he had ruled in favor of Charlie. "Won't you reconsider?"

"That's it. It's over. Go back to work." The words from my father were accented with finality.

"Okay," I added as I opened the door to leave, "but I must add one more piece of information to the story. I told it accurately, but with a twist. I reversed the roles. You've ruled in my favor, not Charlie's, so I'll expect the full commission, not a split. And I don't want to hear any more about it."

I walked out the door with a look of grim satisfaction as my father's face reddened in a combination of anger and pride. He was mad because I had set him up and he'd been had. He was proud because I had taken a stand.

I left as Dad was sputtering. The head salesman laughed. The partner shook his head and seethed. As a result, the rest of the sales staff never messed with me again.

Yes, I got my commission. But Charlie quit and my relationship with my dad's partner was badly bruised. The cost of how I handled it wasn't worth the money I'd made. The ways of the carp are not good ways at all.

My dad and I talked through our situation. He didn't want to be seen as playing favorites and had gone overboard to the other extreme. After realizing what he'd done he never did it again. Our relationship was fine. And after I got serious about the Lord, some eight years later, I wrote Charlie and asked his forgiveness. He gave it, and came to the Lord not too long after, just months before he died. Years later Charlie's son professed Christ as well. It had taken the Lord a long time to work out the consequences from my carp-filled solution to the problem.

I trusted the salesmen to play by the rules because they were my associates. I trusted Charlie because he was the father of my dad's partner and was an older man. I trusted the partner because he was a part of the hierarchy of the business. And I trusted my dad because he was my dad. But, in this instance, they all let me down.

With the little things in life, trust others until they prove they can't be trusted. You may lose some of the things the world says are valuable, but you won't end up a cynic. But with the biggies in life—your virginity, honor, character, and relationships—follow another rule of thumb. Be wise, not naive. Trust, but don't be foolish. And let that deep confidence in a friend be the result of the test of trials and time.

Never trust another person's judgment regarding your salvation. Remember, they do not know your heart. That doesn't mean that wisdom is not to be found in many counselors.[2] But use their words for confirmation, not conclusion.

> *You are not saved because those around you think you are. They do not know your heart.*

I can hear you muttering under your breath right now, "If I can't trust the experts and I can't trust my peers, who can I trust? I'll trust myself!"

Well . . . maybe so, maybe not. Let me explain.

DON'T TRUST YOUR OWN IDEAS

I was talking to a pilot and asked him about flying in

clouds and fog. I'd heard that a plane could be in a dive and the pilot wouldn't know it. He told me that dominant, decisive people have the most difficult time in those situations. You see, their instincts tell them one thing and the instruments tell them another. They swear they are flying straight and level. And they're used to trusting their wits and instincts. However, the console says the plane is in a fifteen-degree dive and is veering to the right. Do you trust you or it? *Folks, the pilots who survive trust the gauges.*

God gave us the gauges, his Holy Bible. It's the best compass there is. And it says when you have a conflict between what you think is right and what the Bible says is right, the one that's right isn't *usually* the Bible. It's always the Bible! If you've decided on your own what it takes to get to heaven—and have disregarded what the Bible says—you are in for trouble. When what you think and what the Bible says are in conflict, put your trust in God, not yourself.

> *Our ideas about salvation can't be trusted.*

A drunk was stretched out in a gutter a number of years ago in Chicago. When the great evangelist D.L. Moody walked by, the boozer exclaimed, "Why, D.L. Moody, you saved me five years ago."

Moody was somber as he replied, "Yes, you look like one of my converts, not one of the Lord's."

Years before, the drunk had gone forward at one of Moody's crusades. He thought that was all you had to do. Moody was rough but set him straight. "Look out! You don't look saved to me," was the essence of Moody's reply.

The drunk had drawn assurance from the act of going forward at the request of a big-time preacher instead of believing on the Lord Jesus Christ. Was he saved? Who knows? Moody didn't think so.

Remember, we are easily deceived. Carp come calling in all kinds of clothing.

Here are a few examples:

Ask someone the question, "Are you a Christian?" The answer often comes back, "Sure, I've always been a Christian." But the Bible tells us we're born separated from God—you must be born again to be a Christian.

"If you speak in tongues you must be saved," may be reassuring words from a friend. But some carp speak in tongues too, so there better be some other evidences of your faith at work.

"You prayed a prayer to ask Jesus into your heart, so everything is okay," are words of assurance. But how does the friend know the condition of this person's heart when he or she prayed? Were there éclairs in their refrigerator?[3] The person may still be a carp.

All these folks may have been sincere—but they may have been sincerely wrong. You can't know you're a Christian because someone says you are. And you can't know you're saved because you feel like it. You can only know you're a believer if you believe according to Scripture.

Do you believe correctly? If you don't, you won't be ready for finals, and you are still a carp.

God does have a final exam and he doesn't grade on the curve. It's a two-part test. We'll start with part one of the test in the next chapter.

WRAP UP

1. Don't put too much trust in what the experts have

to say. There is more wisdom in many counselors than there is in one. Check their conclusions against the unchanging standard of the Word of God.

2. Be careful of listening to your peers unless they have an unusually close walk with the Lord. Again, your final authority is the Bible.

3. You can't trust yourself, either. Your feelings, emotions, and sin nature make your decision suspect. Make the Bible your standard for making life's decision.

4

CARP-KILLING COMMITMENT

The first time I prayed to receive Christ I was in grade school. Occasionally I went to church with a family down the street. But sometimes I went with my mom. One time, during an altar call, Mom asked me to go forward with her. She thought it would provide salvation for me. I went because she asked. We were even baptized together. We both believed in God. We both believed the Bible. She even gave me one. But neither of us were born again. Not then. Our reasons weren't right. We weren't interested in a personal relationship with Christ. We wanted to please each other, not our Heavenly Father.

My mom prayed to receive Christ with me when she was sixty-five, some twenty-six years later. My moment came when I was a sophomore in high school.

Home, during my high school years, was China Lake, a small town in the high desert in southern California ninety miles from Death Valley. It wasn't exactly hell, but you could see it from there. I think if the Lord had a can of deodorant, he'd shoot it right there.

We'll pick up my story when I was 6' 3." I was fourteen years old and weighed a little less than 130 pounds. I know, it was sad. A microphone stand and I had a lot in common in those days. When I put on my striped swimsuit there was just one stripe on the suit. I had to run around in the shower to get wet and I had to be careful of the drain. I could tread water in a test tube. All of the tall, skinny stories applied to me. When you're that size you try to avoid conflict of all kinds. After all, anyone could break you in two.

I was hitchhiking, back when you could do that in relative safety, when a guy picked me up. It was a Friday night. During the course of the six- or seven-minute ride he asked if I'd go to church with him. There were some special meetings he wanted me to attend.

You need to understand something. Church wasn't a part of anything I did. It wasn't something we did as a family. Remember, I came from a broken home. My mom was a hard-core alcoholic by then. My dad had been the town bookie.

Although I can't tell you how I knew it, I was aware that the Bible my mom had given me was special, so I kept it dusted and I didn't set things on it. I believed it, and on rare occasions I'd read it, but church wasn't a part of "my thing."

This guy had just asked me to go to church. I really didn't want to go. But being a conflict avoider, what was I going to do?

I went.

I was sitting eight rows back, on the left side, and the guy who was preaching was a classic fire-and-brimstone man. I don't know if you've ever heard pure fire-

and-brimstone preaching or not, but when this guy opened his mouth he was talking turn or burn. I mean, flip or fry.

He was a serious "change-your-stroke-or-go-down-in-smoke" kind of dude. And when he preached, he flung the words at you, in volleys and salvos. First this human dragon would blow your hair back, then he would suck you forward as he would take a breath, and then he would blow you back again. I just loved the way he said God. He'd shout, "GAAWD," with a guttural "G," a long drawn out "A," and a heavy emphasis on the "D."

As I was getting used to the guy, he quoted a scripture as only he could quote it, screaming, "WE'VE ALL SINNED AND COME SHORT OF THE GLORY OF GOD!"

Although I believed him, I thought, *Some more than others. If this guy wants to meet some people who are into sin, I'll introduce him to some of my buddies at school. Some of them actually do the things I only think about.*

I saw myself as a good kid. I didn't even lie to my folks. Compared to other people I knew, I thought I was one nice guy.

Then the speaker yelled, "AND THE WAGES OF SIN IS DEATH . . . SEPARATION FROM GOD . . . HELL!"

I thought about that. I knew if you committed murder you'd get the electric chair, life in prison, or a lethal injection. If you robbed a gas station you'd get five to ten in the state pen. And, if you lied to your folks you might get your hands slapped, depending on the mood they were in. In other words, there are degrees of punishment to fit the severity of the crime. We've been brought up on that philosophy. Isn't it the basis of our justice system? So, when this guy tells me God punishes all sin with just one punishment (hell) I'm thinking, *That's not fair.*

I know murder is worse than stealing, and stealing is worse than lying. So, how is it God can treat murderers and liars the same way and still be just and loving and all the rest of the things he's supposed to be? How can he treat me like a hardened criminal? It didn't seem right, so he must be an unfair God. Since I wasn't interested in an unfair God, I thought I'd pass on the whole deal.

Then the preacher man says, "Let me tell you something. All sin is the same in God's eyes, because sin is just saying no to God. Negative behavior tells us whether or not we've sinned; what we do or think will show us whether we have said no."

Draw a circle on a pane of glass and put ten pie-shaped wedges in it. Call the wedges the Ten Commandments if you want to. Then take a hammer and try to break your favorite piece of pie. What happens? The whole thing shatters, because you can't punch a hole in a pane of glass with a hammer. When you use a hammer it's impossible to break the glass a little bit. That's the way it is with sin. *You either are a sinner or you're not, because sin can't be done just a little bit.*

Our Lord made it clear, didn't he? He said, "If you've broken one of God's laws, you've broken them all." He went on and said that if you've looked at a woman with lusting eyes you've committed adultery, and if you've looked at a man with anger in your heart you've murdered him. In other words, if you've dwelled on the thought in your head, you've actually done what you thought about.

Although I didn't see myself as a sinner, I had broken a few rules, and I'd thought about breaking a lot of them. It was then that I realized what I was . . . a sinner, separated from God.

Have you ever noticed the eyes in the portraits in the haunted house at Disneyland or Disney World, the ones that follow you as you walk by? Those eyes are watching everyone, but you think they are just watching you. Well, the preacher must have had eyes like that.

He penetrated my soul when he bellowed, "HAVE YOU EVER SAID NO TO GOD?"

His eyes, God's power, my lostness . . . they all converged at once and I blurted out, "Yeaaaah!!!"

What a wonderful day! Oh, it really was, because until you see yourself as a sinner, you just don't perceive your need for a Savior. Until you realize you're separated from God, you just don't see your need to be reconciled to him.

I finally saw my sin. The preacher told me about Christ and asked me to invite him to come into my life. He said that Jesus would do the rest; he would cleanse me, solve my sin problem, reconcile me to God, and make me his child if I would ask him into my life. Hey, I jumped at the opportunity. I even walked down the aisle to the front of the church for the altar call. This time I did it for me. I was a legitimate believer.

Or was I?

In grade school I believed. In high school I believed. And at twenty-nine I believed. When did my belief result in salvation?

COUNTERFEIT BELIEFS

What I'm about to say may surprise you: It is possible to believe that Jesus is the Son of God and that he died for your sins—and still not be a Christian. Belief by itself doesn't do anything for you. A head knowledge of

Christ doesn't solve the problem of sin. James 2:19 says that the demons believe in Christ, but it is not a belief taken to a point of commitment for Jesus. On the contrary, their belief has taken them to a point of opposition. The demons indwelling the man of the tombs of the Gadarenes instantly knew who got out of the boat first.[1] It was the Son of God, and those demons acknowledged the power Jesus had over them. They believed and trembled, but their belief left them lost because it did not include commitment to Christ. Their hearts were like granite.

Pharaoh's heart was hardened after repeatedly refusing the Father's wishes to let his people go. Like the fallen angels, he too had a hard heart that was opposed to turning. But if anyone believed in God it was him. After ten plagues, who wouldn't? However, belief in God doesn't save. Intellectual assent does not equal salvation.

I'm fearful that many people in the church today have a counterfeit belief—it looks like the real thing, but it isn't. It's belief that is placed in the wrong thing. Trout's clothes. If your faith in Christ is based on signs and wonders or your good works or who you know, watch out! This chapter should be a big red flag.

REASON #1: MIRACLES ARE LIKE CHINESE FOOD

> Now while he was in Jerusalem at the Passover Feast, many people saw the miraculous signs he was doing and believed in his name (John 2:23).

Did these people believe unto salvation? The answer is in the next verse:

> But Jesus would not entrust himself to them,

for he knew all men (John 2:24).

Not saved! Their belief was placed in what Jesus did, not in who he is.

> *To be a Christian,*
> *the object of your belief must be Christ.*

These people believed as long as they could observe Jesus' tricks. But when the tricks ended, so did their "belief." Miracles are a lot like Chinese food . . . they don't stay with you very long. You need more right away or you get hungry.

Do you believe because either you or someone you know has spoken prophesies, performed deliverance, or taken part in a miracle? (Those were the issues in Matthew 7.) Look out!

I am not taking a cold shot at those who are charismatic. I speak in both kinds of churches. (Actually, my desire is that after reading this book you might be left wondering, "Does he or doesn't he?") Just remember that the ability to perform miracles, signs, or wonders is not proof of your salvation. There is more than one source of power in the universe, and the enemy is also capable of doing tricks.

> At that time if anyone says to you, 'Look, here is the Christ!' or, 'There he is!' do not believe it. For false Christs and false prophets will appear and perform great signs and miracles to deceive even the elect—if that were possible (Matthew 24:23-24).

It's going to get pretty crazy out there. People who are easily dazzled will be deceived. It will be so bad that solid believers will get rocked. That's why the object of our faith must be The Rock himself, Jesus Christ.

It's wonderful when spiritual power is the by-product of your belief in action. That's the purpose of spiritual gifts. But it's dangerous when power is the object of a person's beliefs.

Jesus died for your sin. His miracles won't save you, but he can. Put your belief in him, not what he did, or what you think he's doing.

REASON #2: WORTHLESS WORKS

Jesus answered, "The work of God is this: to believe in the one he has sent." So they asked him, "What miraculous sign then will you give that we may see it and believe you? What will you do? (John 6:29-30)

Do you think they believed? The answer came in verse 36:

But as I told you, you have seen me and still you do not believe.

It had been a big day. Jesus had fed a multitude and had chased down his disciples on foot while they were boating. Part of that multitude hitched some rides across the sea and hooked up with Jesus on the other side the next day.

These people that Jesus fed the day before came looking for some more fast food. The Lord confronted them with eternity. They countered and showed their lack of understanding by asking, "What shall *we* do." They wanted to know, "What's my part in the deal?" They wanted to know what they had to do to get to heaven.

The answer: believe in Christ alone!

The way a child does it is best. It's uncomplicated. Adults make it so hard. "Watch out for the false teachers who complicate belief," is a message from Jesus, the apostle Paul, and others. They were talking to the people who kept trying to add something to what Jesus did on the Cross. The first time it happened was in Acts 15.

The whole story reminds me of the three clergymen who all purchased new cars. The Baptist minister covered his with water before he drove it. The Catholic sprinkled his. But the Rabbi cut off a piece of his car's tail pipe. That's right, the issue of Acts 15 was circumcision.

The legalistic Jews who had been saved wanted Gentiles who had become Christians to get circumcised. As a matter of fact, they insisted on it. They said you couldn't become a Christian unless you were. Paul threw a fit and the "powers that be" backed off. The bottom line was that it is Christ who saves and Christ alone.

Not only will the enemy try to take your eyes off Jesus, but he will make you believe you can do something to earn your salvation. That's what the Pharisees tried to do.

Here are a few things that won't save you no matter how much trust you place in them:

> Going to church
> Good deeds
> Living by the Golden Rule
> Your denomination
> Prayers
> Calling yourself a "Christian"
> Baptism

Catechism
Attending Sunday school
Memorizing verses
Reading your Bible
Going forward at camp or in church
Infant baptism or dedication
Being a nice person and never having
murdered anyone

A relationship with Jesus requires more than good works. You cannot earn his forgiveness.

> *Good works won't save you;*
> *you must believe in Christ alone.*

REASON #3: "CHRISTIAN" BY ASSOCIATION

I think back to my L.A. Laker days. After a ball game, people who had enough clout could come into the dressing room.

These folks were personalities and friends of friends in high places. They'd hang out around the players. There weren't as many after a loss. Some season ticket holders loved to line the exit onto the floor. They tried to get as close to us as they could. They told people that they knew so-and-so, and they did. But try as they might, they weren't Lakers. They were around us, they associated with us, but they couldn't suit up. They weren't on the team. We called them glad-handers. A lot of Christians are like these people. Jesus encountered some when he was preaching at the treasury inside the temple.

As he spoke, many folks believed. He'd been at it for

a while so some left. He talked further with those who stayed.

> As He spoke these things, many came to believe in Him. Jesus therefore was saying to those Jews who had believed Him, "If you abide in My word, then you are truly disciples of Mine (John 8:30, 31 NAS).

This is an apparently clear and simple passage. "Many came to believe in him" is as straightforward as you can get. Or so it seems.

The Jews of Jesus' day were very aware of their heritage. A chosen race, and they knew it. Parting waters, manna, doves, quail, spouting rocks, pillars, and plagues . . . miracles galore. When God is on your side it's enough to make you cocky— too cocky.

They answered, "We are Abraham's offspring." What they said was, "We are Jews you know. That is our heritage and it is a good one. Jesus is a Jew and we're Jews, we're his people—don't talk to us about sin!"

Jesus' response was a show stopper. "You belong to your father, the devil, and you want to carry out your father's desire."

Wow! There is nothing confusing about the wording: "Many came to believe in him." But they belonged to satan, not God.

Thomas was another who ran with the right crowd—if anyone looked like a believer, he certainly did. After all, he followed Christ for three years. He was as close to him as anybody, except maybe Peter, James, and John. We know he was even willing to go to Jerusalem and die with his main man Jesus. Yet, I don't think he was saved . . . until after the Resurrection.

Here's the scenario. Jesus has died and has been resurrected. Judas had killed himself. The ten were in the upper room. Thomas wasn't with them. (He was off contemplating his navel. . . .) The ten were afraid of the Jews. It's understandable, their leader was gone. So, they locked the door. They didn't want anyone to knock and they didn't want anyone to open it.

Jesus honors their request. He doesn't knock and he doesn't open the door. He just walks in, says peace, and then breathes the Holy Spirit on them. It was a little forty-day blast of the Spirit designed to last until Pentecost.

A person can't have the Holy Spirit unless they're saved. Since Pentecost hadn't occurred yet, the Holy Spirit hadn't been universally given. So, Jesus' breathing the Holy Spirit on the ten proves they were saved men. By itself this occurrence doesn't prove that Thomas wasn't saved—he wasn't there. But it does prove that the ten were born again.

Peter had thought all twelve were believers. He had been the spokesman for the group when he told Jesus, "We believe and know that you are the Holy One of God" (John 6:69). We know he was wrong about Judas . . . it looks like he missed with Tommy, too.

Thomas showed up that evening and one of the ten said, "Tom, my man, you should have been here. It was incredible. Jesus was here!"

"Are you kidding my lips? Are you putting me on? I think you guys are under a lot of stress. This threat by the Jews has really freaked you out. I think you've mass hallucinated or something. What you're suggesting is right out of Star Trek. It's sci-fi at it's best. Guys, what in the world are you saying? I don't believe that. I can't believe it. Unless I can put my finger in the holes in his hands and my hand in his side I'm not going to buy it!

It's too far out!"

My Bible says, "That if you confess with your mouth, 'Jesus is Lord,' and believe in your heart that God raised him from the dead, you will be saved" (Romans 10:9). The opposite is also true. If you don't believe it, you're not. Thomas didn't believe it . . . a carp in trout's clothing.

But let me finish the story. Eight days later Jesus shows up again. Same scenario, only this time Thomas is there. And as Jesus walks through the wall the Savior's eyes lock in on Thomas. As his eyes did their thing, Jesus rotated His side to show Thomas that hole. And he showed him his palms as He spoke. Christ says, "Thomas, Oh, Thomas. Check it out."

Do you remember what Thomas said? He said, "My Lord and my God." Jesus became his Savior . . . and Thomas became a bass.

Tough Tommy had hung around Jesus a long time, just like churchgoers have hung around church for years. Thomas acted like he was a Christian—he probably thought he was. Peter had said he was, hadn't he? Lots of tweeners have been hanging around saved people, but knowing the right people doesn't bring salvation.

Do you relate? Yes, I know you believe. It's doubtful you would have read this far if you didn't, but is something holding you back from a proper belief? Thomas submitted to the lordship of Christ. He expressed it when he said "My Lord and my God." Christ transformed him. Not only did he take off his trout's clothes, he got a new set of scales.

A relationship with Jesus requires more than association. You cannot draw alongside him. He must come inside you. The difference is subtle but it has eternal consequences.

> *Association with Christ won't save you;*
> *you must be a partaker.*

Unlike the folks who fantasize about being a professional basketball player, who cannot because they do not have the physical attributes, everyone can become a child of God. That means that every "Christian" can become a Christian. The keys are the heart and a right belief.

MOTIVES FOR TRUSTING IN CHRIST: FEAR, REWARDS, & LOVE

What motivates saving trust in Christ?

For some it's fear. I don't mean that in the sense of deep reverence either. I mean scared out of your gourd. And that's okay—hell is something to be afraid of: "I don't want to go to hell, so I'll turn to God if I have to!" Fear is also a terrific reason for staying pure, being obedient, and developing Godly character. As Christians we'll never suffer from God's wrath, but his hand of discipline will come on us to the degree that is necessary to break our will.

Knowing Christ also brings some rewards in the here and now: contentment is one. The fruit of the Spirit is another: love, joy, peace, patience, kindness, goodness, faithfulness, gentleness, and self-control. All pretty good reasons to discover the right kind of belief in Jesus Christ. Add to that the unknown hierarchy of the rewards in heaven that will be ours, and you've got some legitimate personal reasons to pursue Christ. And they are all okay with God—he dangled them in front of us.

Of course the best and purest motive for getting to know God is the result of your deep love for him and your gratitude for what Christ did for you. When acts of obedient service and impromptu worship come out of a heart so filled with love that it can't be contained, you've got the best situation imaginable. Folks, that's worth chasing after! God says do it.

WHAT KIND OF BELIEF SAVES?

I can hear you now . . . Okay Jay, you've told me some things I may have confused for true belief. How can I know if my belief is the kind that saves?

Let me answer that by telling you a story. I was in Disneyland one summer and got to see what's left of the Great Wallendas. They were a family of circus tightrope walkers who were the best the world has ever seen. Some years ago they were involved in an accident that killed several of them. Only a few are still performing.

This fellow and his wife had stretched a tight wire across Main Street at the entrance into the park. I sat and watched him go back and forth in various ways wearing those little sissy slippers. With his balancing bar he rode a bike across and back, did a flip, and even jumped rope. I put the sissy stuff out of my head when I saw him spread his legs, fall to the wire, and rebound to his feet. The trick made me wince and take a deep breath. Then he took a wheelbarrow, put his wife in it, and slowly wheeled across the wire. It was a great trick and I saw him do it.

Do you believe someone could push a person across a tight rope in a wheelbarrow? Do you think he really did it? Sure, he even does it across canyons; that guy is really good. Do you believe? Probably. But would you get in the wheelbarrow? Me neither. I believe he can do it, but I'm not gonna let him do it with me. I believe, but I lack commitment because I'm not going to get into the wheelbarrow.

Commitment. What a word! It's a word of division. It's a decision that separates the men from the boys and the women from the girls. It separates true belief from false belief.

When belief is true belief, there is a turning to God (repentance), a selling out; there is a commitment and an allegiance to Christ that is sufficient to change behavior. Commitment, when coupled with belief, is the hop into Christ's wheelbarrow.

Is your belief placed in Christ alone—
or have you relied on counterfeit evidence
for your assurance of salvation?

FOLLOW ME

Jesus said to Matthew, "Follow me."[2] Most of the folks who heard him thought he meant "go where I go."

But that wasn't what Jesus wanted. He was saying, "Have a change of heart so that you can stop being like you and start becoming like me. Don't just die. Anyone can do that." Jesus wanted them to start the process of dying to self and allow the Spirit of God to develop Christlike character qualities in them. A person has to repent, commit, and declare allegiance to do that. That's the result of a changed heart. It's the component that turns "belief" into belief.

Belief that results in salvation embraces repentance, allegiance, and commitment. Its more than just turning from sin, it also includes a drawing alongside of Christ and a desire to do what he says. A person who just "believes" has a head knowledge of Christ but isn't sold out. Belief without repentance is like kissing your sister. (It doesn't do anything for you.)

REPENTANCE: ABOUT FACE

Imagine people walking away from God. As they are walking, their pace slows and they come to a stop. Some turn and face God, some keep on walking. Of those who turn, some start forward at various speeds (from crawling to sprinting), while others stand still. The people who have turned have had a change of heart . . . they have repented.

Some of those who turn begin running toward God, others walk, but a few don't move at all. Some of the runners and walkers are on the inside lane of an Olympic track and they move quickly while others stumble over every hurdle. Others are in the Sierras backpacking in shale, going backward two steps for every step forward. The way you are moving will affect your spiritual power, but it won't affect your position in Christ— because of the direction you are facing.

Which way are you facing?

The walkers were facing toward God, and that's the key to salvation. They turned . . . they had a change of heart, and with the turning they demonstrated their belief in God through Jesus Christ to the point of saving faith. They hopped in the wheelbarrow.

Saving faith = belief demonstrated in a change of heart.

What about those who turned and didn't move? I don't know . . . and neither do they.

Perhaps some frogs on a log will drive this point home.

Five frogs were on a log, four decided to jump. How many are left? Did you say one? Allow me to nitpick. Deciding to jump and jumping are two different decisions. And the second will determine the validity of the first.

For example, I have decided to go to the store to buy some deodorant on my way home from work tonight. But the fellas on the job ask me to hang out with them at the day's end. Do I go to the store or hang with the guys? My next decision will demonstrate the validity of my first decision. If I go with the fellas I didn't really decide to get the deodorant.

If you call yourself a Christian, does your behavior validate your decision to receive Christ?

Are you sold out for Jesus . . . a "kick carp" bass?

Are you somewhere in between . . . a trout?

Or are you a nonbeliever . . . a carp?

If you've answered yes to either of the last two—or you're not sure—read on. It's time to test the waters. This is where the carp hits the fan.

WRAP UP

1. It's possible to believe and not be saved.
2. Proper belief must have a proper object. The object of energizing faith is Jesus Christ.
3. We can't be good enough to qualify for heaven. God doesn't grade on the curve.
4. Association with Christianity and Christians does not make you a Christian. Christianity occurs through a relationship with Christ.
5. Fear, rewards, and responses in love are all acceptable motives.
6. Belief has to embrace repentance, allegiance, and commitment.

5

TESTING THE WATERS

I'm from Missouri. And I'm as stubborn as a Missouri mule. You thought as much, and you were correct.

We have some traditional Missouri Ozark sayings in our household. They come from my dad. "Blinking like a toad in a hailstorm" is one. "Screaming like a smashed cat" is another. Or how about "Being as nervous as a long-tailed cat in a room full of rockers"?

Missouri is the "show me" state. "The proof is in the puddin' " is a saying that must have originated there. In Missouri the bottom line is the bottom line. Talk's cheap. Missourians reserve their judgment until they see action.

God must be from Missouri. He said that faith without works is dead.[1] In other words, if you're a Christian it ought to show.

One of the greatest days of my life came as a junior higher when I came home from school, depressed again. The kids had been talking about what their dads did for a living. My dad was a bookmaker and made his living bookin' horses and running a poker parlor.

When my father asked me what was wrong, I told him of my embarrassment regarding what he did. It was a Friday.

My dad was an honest gambler. So honest, in fact, his poker chips were legal tender at most of the markets and restaurants in our little town. He would make the rounds every Wednesday to redeem his chips.

But that Friday he gave his notice. On Monday he collected all his chips, settled up, and began a legitimate business from which he would retire ten years later.

I never had to ask if my dad loved me. He gave up thousands of dollars a week, back when a thousand dollars was a lot of money. And he did it for the respect of his son and out of his love for him. He didn't just tell me he loved me, he showed it. The proof of his love was in what he did.

How much do dads who never show love to their sons or daughters really love them? Nobody knows. Neither the dad nor the child. Only God. Lip service is not proof. And in salvation, actions speak louder than words. The proof is in the puddin'.

If you love God it should show, shouldn't it? Who knows how much a person loves God? Unless it shows, only God, and that's pretty scary because if the person doesn't know, how can they possibly have peace about eternity?

How does a believer demonstrate his or her faith? I'll tell you in a minute when we test the waters. But first, let me take you on a brief digression (I've always wanted to write one of those!). It will help you evaluate the fruit in your life.

PRACTICERS ARE LOST

There is a terrifying concept in 1 John 3:

"The one who practices sin is of the devil"(8a NAS). "No one who is born of God practices sin" (9a NAS)

Do you still sin? Me, too. There are a couple of things I've been working to overcome for years. A little lingering carp. Am I a practicer of sin? If I am, I'm not a Christian.

A look at King David's life helps us understand what this means. The monarch probably raped Bathsheba, committed adultery, commissioned a murder, and was nonrepentant for at least two years, until his confrontation with God through the prophet Nathan.

He looks like a carp to me. What do you think?

If I were David's fruit inspector I would have judged him to be a practicer. Rape, adultery, and murder are biggies. And two years is a long time. My conclusion would be "not saved." But notice, David never lost his sense of conscience for his sin. And he knew God's forgiving nature. One result was Psalm 51, a great statement of repentance. Perhaps the greatest. It's all summarized in verses 10-13:

> Create in me a pure heart, O God, and renew a steadfast spirit within me. Do not cast me from your presence or take your Holy Spirit from me. Restore to me the joy of your salvation and grant me a willing spirit, to sustain me. Then I will teach transgressors your ways, and sinners will turn back to you.

In spite of his sin David had a deep-down desire to please God. The Father had put his Spirit in him.[2]

There are two sources for conscience. The Spirit of God and your moral upbringing. You can't make the Holy Spirit go away. But you can influence your moral conscience. The following story illustrates what I mean.

Grace and Ted were both divorced. Having been raised in moral, Christian homes, they knew right from wrong. Both claimed to be Christians.

The pair had met at a singles' function at their church. They began to date and were strongly attracted to each other. Knowing it was wrong, they let passion prevail, and had sex together. Both felt guilt.

Being lonely yet not wanting to get burned again, they weren't yet ready to remarry, so they moved in together. Time had desensitized Grace. She no longer felt any pangs of conscience. Ted, on the other hand, couldn't get over his guilt. He wasn't committed to God enough to move out, but couldn't find any peace either. Is the Spirit of God within Grace? Perhaps, but not likely. It's doubtful that she's born again. The jury is still out on Ted, because he doesn't know if his lingering conscience is the result of his moral upbringing or the Holy Spirit.

Both Grace and Ted were iffy. Trout! Both may be bass dressed up as trout—but Grace is probably a carp. Who knows about Ted?

You can't alter the conscience of the Holy Spirit. And that's the key. If you don't feel guilty about your sin, you are probably not saved. Your conscience is not evidence of salvation, because it might be the result of your upbringing and environment. However, not having a conscience is a strong indication that the Holy Spirit is absent.

David sinned for a season, but its clear from Psalm 51 that David wasn't a practicer of sin. (I call him a stumbler.) He was a bass in trout's clothing. When the Spirit of God is at work, you have evidence of who's living in the temple we call your body.[3] The Spirit's presence is an index of salvation, making the sinner a stumbler, not a practicer. His presence is one of the ways to test the waters.

WATCH OUT FOR THE TRICKSTER

As you test your faith, keep in mind that the deceiver is very good at imitating and counterfeiting the Spirit of God. Feelings and experiences aren't always trustworthy. The devil can demonstrate power just as God's Spirit can, and he is capable of making you think "the juice" is from the Father. People speak in tongues in the Church of Satan, which is evidence of the devil being capable of duplicating that gift. They practice other sign gifts as well, including healing.

The proof of his presence in you is your faith in the promises of God's holy Word. Do you or do you not believe what the Bible says about Jesus Christ? Knowing he's for real is about the only way you can be sure—as long as your belief is coupled with a heart for God. It's clear, if you know Jesus Christ, the deal's been sealed with the Holy Spirit.[4] And if he's there, you should see the fruit of the Spirit in the form of love, joy, peace, patience, kindness, goodness, faithfulness, gentleness and self-control.[5] It's time to take the test.

ARE YOU READY FOR FINALS?

The test for salvation is to be found in 1 John 5:13:

> These things I have written to you who believe
> in the name of the Son of God, in order that
> you may know that you have eternal life.
> (NAS)

"These things" refers to the book of 1 John.[6] In other words, if you dissect John's first letter you should be able to tell if you have eternal life. For simplicity's sake I have reduced the criteria into six categories. There are others, but these are the biggies.

Keep in mind that if you are in the middle of a stumble it may be difficult for you to take this test. David would have had trouble prior to Nathan's arrival, too. Just remember, evaluate your life on the basis of how you were when you became a Christian and how you are now. If there is no difference between then and now, it doesn't mean you aren't saved, but it is a waving red flag that strongly suggests you should check it out.

The Bible tells us to:

> Examine yourselves to see whether you are in the faith; test yourselves. Do you not realize that Christ Jesus is in you—unless, of course, you fail the test? (2 Corinthians 13:5)

So, let's do it. Take the following test.

TEST NO. 1: *Are you more aware of God than you used to be?*[7]

Has your reverence and dependence on him increased with time? Is his holiness affecting the way you live your life? Do you have a desire to learn more about him and draw closer? Or is God still just "the man upstairs" or some "cosmic constrainer?"

If things between you and God are about the same as they've always been, the red flag is waving. Look out!

TEST NO. 2: *Has your relationship with Jesus Christ deepened?*[8]

Do you have an increasing understanding of the power that was demonstrated in the Resurrection? Is there a growing sense of awe over what he did for you, personally? Is it bothering you more and more when you hear his name used as a swear word? Or is Christ still just a man who lived a couple of thousand years ago whose name is tagged on to your "now I lay me down to sleep" token prayers?

If your relationship with Jesus Christ hasn't deepened and become more personal over the years, the red flag is waving a warning. Check it out!

TEST NO. 3: *Is the Bible progressively becoming the standard by which you make your life's decisions?*[9]

Is the Bible the hallmark for what's right and wrong for you? Are you progressively trusting it over your own sense of right and wrong? Or is it that book over there with a layer of dust on it that you occasionally read with a hunt and peck method?

If you are still living as you please instead of more as the Bible instructs, the red flag is waving. You probably have a problem!

TEST NO. 4: *Do you hate sin more than you used to?*[10]

Do you find yourself hating the little things that didn't used to bother you? Do you have a progressively growing hatred of sin? Does the carp in your life bug you more and more? Or are things pretty much the way they've always been regarding your behavior?

If your life isn't holier now than before coming to Christ, you've got problems. Not being saved may likely be one of them!

TEST NO. 5: *Are you a little bit more like Jesus than you used to be?*[11]

To your surprise, as you look back, do you find that you aren't as selfish as you used to be? There aren't as many people you don't like, and there are more that you do. Are you more forgiving, caring, loving? Can you honestly say, "I am a little bit more like Jesus?" Or, are things about the same. Are you still looking out for number one (you) as much as ever?

If you are not a little bit more like Jesus, the red flag is waving. Something's not right!

TEST NO. 6: *Do you have the awareness of the Holy Spirit in your life?*[12]

This one can be kinda tricky. It is true that you can't be trusted, so convictions are not proofs, they are evidences. Moonies, Jehovah's Witnesses, and Mormons all have convictions. But a deep unwavering confidence that doesn't roller coaster with emotion or circumstance can be a pretty good test of where you are, if you also see evidence of the other signs.

DID YOU PASS?

How did you do? Are you aware of Jesus Christ working in your life? Have some things been happening? Is your life changing? Did you pass?

If you got an F and realize you don't know Christ as Savior and you want to know him, turn to pages 118-123 and 131-133 to find out how to pray to receive him into your life.

If you realize that Christ isn't in your life, and you didn't turn to page 118, let me tell you about my friend Dick.

I met Dick while playing AAU basketball for the Kitchen Fresh Chippers, a potato chip manufacturer. He coached the team. I wasn't into the Lord much in those days, but occasionally I'd have flashes of spirituality. Dick had been raised in church and had a highly committed and godly wife. As a result, Dick knew all the Christian buzz words.

I'd asked him if he was a believer. His response was, "Not yet, I still have a few things I want to do. After I do them I'll accept him."

After my decision to serve God, Dick's words still burned in my heart. I tracked him down and gave him a call. After the usual hellos, the conversation went something like this:

"Dick, have you received Christ yet?"

"No, not yet, but I'm close."

"What's keeping you?"

"A couple more things to do."

"Is it true that you believe everything the Bible says about Jesus?"

"Yes, absolutely."

"But you won't ask him into your life."

"Not yet."

It was then I posed a hypothetical question. "Dick, what if a truck was coming straight at you on the freeway and a head-on collision was unavoidable?"

"I'd quick pray and receive Christ."

"What if it happened from the rear and you didn't have time to pray?"

His reply totally caught me off-guard. "That's a chance I'm willing to take for a while."

"You understand and believe, yet you are willing to toy with eternity because you're not ready to make a commitment? Dick, I don't understand such thinking."

"That's the way it is."

I called my friend every year for four years. The fourth call found him a believer and wondering how a person could be such a fool to have been willing to play such a dangerous game of Russian roulette with life.

Are you playing Russian roulette? Do you know you're not saved? Then I urge you to turn to page 115.

If you got anything less than an A, it doesn't mean you're not saved. But it does mean you are swimming around in Tweener's Bog. The murky waters of the fuzzy gray. And nobody but God knows the condition of the fish in that pond.

I hope reality got your attention. As a trout, it's tough to have assurance of your salvation.

Why be lukewarm? Read on. The last two chapters will help change your trout's clothes and might even change your scales.

WRAP UP

1. The proof of your salvation will be in the puddin' of your life.
2. Practicers of sin are lost, stumblers are saved.
3. Practicers have lost their sense of conscience for their sin.
4. Signs and doubts have more than one source and must be checked out. They are not always evidence of the Holy Spirit in action.
5. There are at least six primary salvation criteria from 1 John that are progressive in nature: (1) Growing relationship with God; (2) Growing relationship with Jesus Christ; (3) Deepening commitment to the Bible; (4) Progressive hatred of sin; (5) Becoming a little bit more like Jesus; (6) Confirming presence of the Holy Spirit.

6

TURN AND BURN YOUR CARP, FLIP AND FRY YOUR FISH

I have a friend who was a fighter pilot in World War II. During his training he flew planes that didn't have radios. That's the way it was in those days. Signal men on the ground communicated with the young flyers by waving flags.

Bill was the best in his class and had a chance to prove it during the graduation exercises. With the grandstands full of top brass, sweet William set out to make a mark for himself. He won the touch-and-go competition easily, captured first place in the dog-fight event, and thereby won the right to land first.

Bill was feeling fine. Top Gun, that's who he was. And he was leading the parade. As he was enjoying his victory his thoughts went to making a perfect landing just to cap off a perfect day of flying. He thought about the applause awaiting him as he climbed out of his plane.

My friend lowered his flaps as he started his approach. A buzzer started buzzing in the cockpit. Bill knew what it meant but was so caught up in the moment that it didn't register. He could see the men in the tower waving with both hands. "Hi guys," he yelled knowing they couldn't hear him. *How nice of them to welcome the conquering hero.* Then a red flare sailed across his vision. *Fireworks for the winner.* They had thought of everything.

Concentrate, concentrate. Focus on making both wheels touch at the same time.

As the plane settled to the ground Bill noticed the propeller stop. This phenomenon was followed by the screech of metal. The propeller had stopped because it had hit the ground. The ear-piercing sound was caused by the body of the plane doing the same thing. As a cloud of dust enveloped the plane Bill remembered, *I forgot to put down the landing gear, I didn't lower the wheels.*

Bill thought he was a winner. He thought everything was just fine . . . until it was too late.

Oh, he'd been warned. The buzzer was installed as a reminder to the pilot to put his gear down whenever the flaps were lowered. The guys in the tower tried to wave him off. The red flare was an attempt to keep him from landing.

But Bill crashed.

And now it was too late. Nothing more could be done.

This book is a friend in the tower trying to wave you off. It's a final flare. It just might be your last warning buzzer. Get your wheels down. Don't crash, you need to be born again.

A few presidential terms ago the words *born again* got bruised pretty badly. The phrase was seen on the fronts of national newspapers, the cover of weekly magazines, and was broadcast over the radio air waves, as well as T.V. Any time you hand over a concept to the media, you'll lose its meaning for sure. We have even denominationalized the concept to the point that some churches don't even know what it means.

Let's go back to the Bible and try to accomplish two things in this chapter: (1) figure out what Jesus meant when he said, "You must be born again"; (2) help you stake your claim that you are born again, if, in fact, you are.

How can you be born again? Nobody knows—but you can know if it's happened to you.

I preach a message entitled "Born Again, It Ain't What It Used to Be." In it I present several analogies as an attempt to communicate the concept of being born again.

THE WIND

Pharisees were corrupt, hypocritical, office-seeking legalists. Jesus called them snakes and vipers. He didn't think much of them. They were so legalistic you couldn't walk on the grass on the Sabbath because you might knock some grass seed loose, and if it hit the ground it would be construed as planting. Since you weren't allowed to plant on the Sabbath there was no walking on the grass on the Sabbath. We're talkin' serious legalism.

The main character of John 3 is Nicodemus, a Pharisee and a ruler of the Jews. As a member of the Sanhedrin, his position was similar to a senator's. Perhaps he was even the head honcho.

As a Pharisee, Nicodemus could be known as Rabbi, Pastor, or as a Doctor of Divinity. As the ruler of the Jews he might be referred to as Your Honor, Judge,

Professor, or Senator. Nicodemus was a high-powered guy, a real big shot, and he had several hats he could wear.

> He came to Jesus at night and said, "Rabbi, we know you are a teacher who has come from God. For no one could perform the miraculous signs you are doing if God were not with him" (John 3:2).

Notice he said *we*. Has he got a frog in his pocket? What's the deal? Nicodemus is alone, but he says we. It's because he's put on his Pharisee hat. He's coming to Jesus representing the Pharisees.

And he comes at night. Why? Jesus might have been too busy to see him that day. Or, he might have been too busy to see Jesus. But, most likely he didn't want any of his buddies to see him.

So, Nicodemus comes to Jesus and in effect says, "I know God is with you, so you must know all about the things of God. I mean, nobody can do the kind of tricks you do unless God is with him." But what he was really asking was, "How can I know for sure that I'm in the kingdom of God? I'm working really hard as a Pharisee to get in, but I'm not sure it's hard enough. How hard is hard enough?"

In response, Jesus hits him up along the side of his head with a verbal two-by-four: "I tell you the truth, no one can see the kingdom of God unless he is born again."

Jesus knocked off Nicodemus's Pharisee hat when he said, "Talk about the kingdom of God. Why Nicodemus, you're not even gonna see it because to get there you must be born again—and you're not."

But the man wasn't a senator for nothin'. He was

quick on his feet and showed it with his comeback as he switched hats:

> "How can a man be born when he is old?" Nicodemus asked. "Surely he cannot enter a second time into his mother's womb to be born!" (John 3:4).

Nicodemus does the old soft-shoe two-step and comes at Jesus one more time. "Hey, I'm a grown man. I can't go back into my mother's womb. Jesus, what in the world are you talking about?"

The Lord cleared it up some with his reply:

> Jesus answered, "I tell you the truth, no one can enter the kingdom of God unless he is born of water and the Spirit. Flesh gives birth to flesh, but the Spirit gives birth to spirit. You should not be surprised at my saying, 'You must be born again' "(John 3:5-7).

Jesus had just told Nicodemus that he was a two-part critter. There was one part, the part he could see, touch, and smell—the physical part. But there was another part, the spiritual dimension—his soul. When this body can no longer house it, our soul goes someplace else. And unless your soul has a birth, just as you had a physical birth, you'll spend eternity separated from God. You must be born again. Your soul must undergo birth.

What happens when spiritual birth takes place? It's a good question:

> The wind blows wherever it pleases. You hear its sound, but you cannot tell where it comes from or where it is going. So it is with everyone born of the Spirit (John 3:8).

When you feel the wind, are you aware of where it's coming from? Directionally, yes. But where did it come from? You don't know. All you know is that the wind is blowing. You don't know where it came from, and you don't know where it went. But it is blowing, you're sure of that.

Jesus makes it clear. Being born again is a mystery. You can't understand it.

How do you explain ice cream to someone who has never seen a refrigerator, who lives at the equator? Describe cold to someone who has never experienced it. Impossible.

You say: "Ice cream is milk that is all together in a lump."

They reply: "I've seen and smelled *that* before and it's not something I want to eat—even if you make it cold—whatever that is."

You see, it can't be done.

We can't explain the process, but one thing is clear: *We must be born again.*

Jesus said, "I am the way and the truth and the life. No one comes to the Father except through me."[1] How we come to Christ may differ, but there is only one way: spiritual birth.

It's happening to Nicodemus. Puzzled, he asks, "How can this be?"

Ol' Nicodemus didn't know what was going on. He's not Judge Nicodemus, Your Honor Nicodemus, Rabbi Nicodemus, Pastor Nicodemus, Professor Nicodemus, or Doctor of Divinity Degree Nicodemus. Right about then he was just Nic.

But even Nic doesn't satisfy Jesus. That's still a little too highfalutin for him. So the Lord pounds on him a little more to bring out the faith of a child: "You are

Israel's teacher," said Jesus, "and do you not understand these things?"

To come to the Lord he'll have to come as Nicky. Jesus reduces him to that. He's been humbled—and now he's teachable, so the Lord starts teachin' (I'm paraphrasing): "I really know what I'm talkin' about, but you aren't listening. If you're struggling with the basics, how are you ever going to grasp the deeper things of God? I've been to heaven and back. If anybody knows what they're talkin' 'bout, it's me."

Then Christ comes out of left field with two verses that seem strange to us, but actually told Ol' Nic how to believe:

> Just as Moses lifted up the snake in the desert, so the Son of Man must be lifted up, that everyone who believes in him may have eternal life (John 3:14, 15).

Being a good Jew, and well read, Nicodemus knew what Jesus was referring to—God used it on his people when he had Moses put a bronze snake on a stick.[2]

THE STICK

In Moses' day every time the children of Israel messed up, God would lay a heavy on them and then make 'em take another lap (around Mt. Sinai). That would get their attention, so they solicited Moses to pray and ask God to lighten up. Moses would, and God would, and the people were fine until they messed up again. That's the way it went for forty years. (When God told them to take a lap, it took about a year to run it. Forty laps equaled forty years.)

One day the folks expressed their dislike for the fast food they'd been getting free for years. They were sick of the spiritual Big Macs—manna—and began grumbling.

God didn't like their attitude, and he presented them with a few mood modifiers in the way of little red snakes. And every time one bit somebody, that somebody died.

The people called to Moses and said, "Boy have we blown it this time! Go and pray like crazy. Ask God to lighten up. This is the heaviest heavy he's ever laid on us."

So Moses prayed . . . and prayed . . . and prayed.

"People!" Moses called the children of Israel together to hear what God had to say. "I've got good news and bad news. First, the bad news. God's not gonna get rid of the snakes."

As the people gasped, Moses continued, "Yes, I know that's a bummer, but in the past, every time God has removed our problems we have stopped turning to him. It seems that without problems we tend to rely on ourselves. So God, in his wisdom, has chosen to leave us with difficulties, because they tend to drive us back to himself."

Did you ever wonder why we have problems? Wonder no longer. We're no different than the Israelites. Without difficulties we trust in ourselves. Problems force us to the Father.

Moses continued his report, "But there is good news. God told me to make a bronze snake and put it on a stick and place it in the middle of camp. Then if anyone is bitten by a snake, if he or she will look at the snake on the stick, that person won't die. Folks, that's very good news. God has given us a spiritual snakebite kit."

Strangely enough there were four responses to God's message through Moses. The first was by the people who didn't believe in God. I call them pillar doubters. They attributed the pillar of fire at night and the pillar of cloud by day to natural phenomena. They even thought the Red Sea routine was a lucky break. People who have steeled their hearts against the possibility of miracles have a lot of trouble ever seeing the Father.

One day a pillar doubter was bitten by a sneaky slinker. He thought about what to do. *Now let's see. Everyone who is bitten by a snake dies. I know I'm supposed to look at the snake on the stick in the middle of camp, but that's so silly. I think I will use the power within me to will the venom out of my system. My will will save me.* The result: he died.

The second group of people believed in God, but they didn't take him at his word. They couldn't imagine him being for real by only offering one solution to snakebite. *There most certainly must be multiples of solutions* was their belief.

A slippery slitherer chomped on one of these partial believers. *Ouch! I've been bitten by a snake. God wants me to look at the stick, but I hate doing what God wants me to do. Besides, it's hard to believe there is only one way to solve the problem of snakebite. People must be smart enough to solve the problem themselves. Surely there are multiples of ways to cure snakebite. As a matter of fact, I've heard about several solutions from the East.* So he bought a Hare Krishna snakebite kit—and died.

The third group thought they'd get away from the crimson critters by taking off over the hill. But that was a dumb move, because the snakes were out there too. One of the runners was gnawed on and turned to look at the stick. But there was a hill in the way. He had gotten too far away, couldn't see it, and died.

It was the fourth group who did it God's way. One of them was nabbed by a nipper. "Yugga mugga! that hurts," he screamed. "I've been bitten by a snake! Where's the stick?"

He looked—and lived.

Imagine yourself in church on Sunday morning with your congregation. Someone locks the doors and turns three hundred little red snakes loose. The women are getting their feet off the floor. But it won't help because those little suckers can jump. Everyone will be bitten before they get out. Actually everyone had been bitten before they'd arrived.

Our Heavenly Father gave us a picture of what was to come in Numbers 21. The story of snakebite is an illustration of sin. Romans 3:23 makes it clear that we all have been bitten by it. We have all sinned. God put Christ on a stick to solve the problem.

But there are four responses. Some people don't believe there is a God and they deny the Bible as being his Book of Instructions. They refuse to look at Christ on the cross. But, if my Bible is correct (and I certainly believe it is), they are going to hell.

Others think there are several ways besides belief in Christ to solve the sinfulness of man. But if my Bible is accurate, they are going to hell, too.

Some people get too far away, and God hardens their heart. It happened to Pharaoh. It happens today. If I were to speak to a thousand high school people, I would expect seventy-five to one hundred decisions for salvation. If I were to speak to a thousand retired people, I would expect two or three decisions. Why? The older people have spent a lifetime denying the Lord, and every time a person does that, the heart hardens a little. Unless my Bible is wrong, hearts that are hard to God are going to hell.

But the people who obediently look to the Cross will

be saved, if their look goes beyond intellectual scrutiny.

Hold it, I didn't say Christ won't withstand intellectual scrutiny. He most certainly will. But the person who studies the Savior with their head won't solve the problem of sin in their heart—unless the heart changes. Remember, a head knowledge of Christ is like kissing your sister. Belief has to move from the head to the heart. That's a twelve-inch drop on you. It's eighteen inches on me (remember, I'm 6' 8" tall). But if it stays in your head it doesn't do a thing for you.

Jesus said he is knocking on the doors of unbelieving hearts pleading to come in.[3] The essence of his plea is, "Look! With all the adamancy I possess, I want to come into your life." Belief is your hand turning the door knob. Your response to a changed heart is the opening of the door. You can't open the door if you don't turn the knob, and just turning the knob won't open the door. But when the door opens, Christ does the rest.

STAKING YOUR CLAIM

As you work out your salvation with fear and trembling[4] don't make the mistake of letting someone else give you the assurance of your salvation, including me. I've said that before, but it's worth repeating. *Salvation is not something you want to take a chance on.* Taking somebody else's word for it is taking too big a chance. If they're wrong, you could end up in hell.

Do you want to live a life that is pleasing to God? That's the result of a changed heart. It's commitment, repentance, and allegiance. Knowing that you will fail to live up to your desire to bring glory to the Father doesn't lessen the intensity of your desire—and God is concerned with your heart.

Did you say yes? My friend, unless you're kidding

yourself, stake your claim. You're saved.

If you said yes to the above question, yet still lack assurance, turn to pages 131 through 138. I'll suggest some possible causes.

Let me ask you again. *Do you want to please God with your life?* Enough to get rid of the carp in your life and sell out to Christ? That's what bondslaves do.

WRAP UP

1. We don't know what happens when we are born again, but we can know that we are.
2. Salvation comes only through Jesus Christ who died on the cross. We must look to Him, and Him alone.

7

BONDSLAVES ARE "KICK-CARP" BASS

Visualize a low-ceilinged room with a dusty, sooty atmosphere. The floor is dirt and men have been walking about. Dust hangs in the air. Oil lamps on the walls have added their residue as well. The small openings in the walls that serve as windows produce laserlike shafts of sunlight probing diagonally across the room.

The slaves are tethered with leather thongs and are gathered in the front corner. The auctioneer is on the other side. The auction block is front and center. The men are gathered out front. It is slave-trading day.

There are two men you should know about. The one in the front row, over by the slaves, is the worst of the lot. He is cruel beyond words. His pleasure is derived from beating a slave, scourging, skinning, dismembering, and killing him as slowly as he can, while inflicting as much pain as possible. This is his singular joy in life.

The other man is sitting toward the back on the right. He is a Roman prince, older, who is known to be kind and gentle. He treats his slaves like his own children. Those who are fortunate enough to find their way into his household are protected, loved, and nurtured.

The auctioneer has just auctioned off a tall, forty-nine-year-old man. He was a gladiator of sorts when he was younger. His hands are soft, he has a chronic sore back, and he is only good for talking. He didn't sell for much. Old athletes weren't worth much in those days either.

A beautiful seventeen-year-old girl starts to shuffle to the block. Her ankles are tied together with thongs, and the leather around her wrists binds her hands together, drawing her shoulders forward. She stares without expression over the heads of the men who stand before her.

The men sit up, interested. She'll bring a good price. The girl is very lovely indeed.

The bidding is brisk. She doesn't flinch or change her gaze. Until *he* bids—the cruel man. Although the girl doesn't look at him, the corner of her mouth and a muscle twitch in her neck give her away. *Oh no, I hope he's not interested in me!*

As the bidding continues, the wicked taskmaster bids again. She looks in his direction, disbelieving and shaking her head slowly back and forth, her lips silently forming the word no.

He grins, leers, and ups his offer.

A voice from the back of the room. The girl strains to see. The Roman prince. *Are you interested in me? Oh, please be interested in me.*

Hope is shattered by a nod from the front row. It's restored by a gesture from the back. And on and on it went. Back and forth.

Everyone else drops out of the bidding. The girl begins to sob. There will be no in between for her. Only one of the two extremes. Pride is long gone. Fear rules.

Finally, the taskmaster makes a bid and the benevolent Roman doesn't counter.

"Going . . . going . . ."

The girl's eyes are riveted on the gavel as it rises to its apex and starts down. The letter g forms on the lips of the auctioneer. Her face tells the story. Total resignation.

But as the hammer descends, the man in the back yells "Stop! I will make one more bid." To everyone's astonishment the prince names an amount that exceeds the total net worth of the wicked man.

Two statements had been made: "This auction's over, Jack!" and "You're outta your league!"

The wicked man slams his ledger books closed and storms out of the room. The prince comes forward, taking off his cloak as he walks. He puts it around the naked girl and cuts the bindings off each wrist and ankle. Sheltering her with his arm he shouts to the auctioneer so that all in the room can hear, "Prepare a declaration of freedom. Today this girl is free."

The men are stunned. Such a sum had never been paid for a slave before! And to pay it and then declare her free—why, that was unheard of!

"And make her a Roman princess. It is within my power to bestow such a rank."

"What! I don't believe it! He's nuts!"

"And furthermore, she shall be a full heir of a portion of my inheritance. Prepare the document, melt the wax." He presses his signet ring into the hardening wax on the document. He hands the paper to the girl.

She takes the parchment, shaking her head. "No." As her conviction grows she says it again, "NO! I can't!" Looking up at the man she continues, "You paid a price for me that was far greater than has ever been paid. And you saved me from a fate far worse than anything I could ever imagine. I will become your bondslave."

If a Jew had to sell himself into slavery to pay his debts, he had to serve seven years. But then he had the option of going free. However, if he preferred his master's household he could reject his freedom and stay a slave. This privilege occurred once and only once. If he rejected his freedom, he was taken to the door of his master's home, his ear was placed in the door jam and the door shut. This cauliflowered the ear, branding him with the mark of his master's door, connoting final ownership. His ear was then pierced and a ring was inserted. He was now a bondslave.

A slave had to serve, but a bondslave had chosen to serve. And he would never again have the option of his freedom. It signaled an irrevocable decision. The slave had totally sold out to serving his master, willingly and without coercion. There was no going back.

When Paul, Peter, James and others said they were *bondslaves* of Christ, they were saying a mouthful. It was a gesture of grateful response measured by total sell-out.

A GESTURE OF GRATEFUL RESPONSE

Do you understand what Jesus Christ died to save us from? Hell! Our sins would send us there apart from him. And our minds cannot comprehend what that would be like. We cannot fathom the awfulness of that place. Although the Bible tells us a bit about it, we don't really have a clue as to how bad it will be for those who go there. If we did, we wouldn't let our friends go there without putting up more of a fight.

It will be a bona fide carp fry.

Flip the coin for a moment. Can you grasp the magnitude of the payment made to save you from the pit?

If you were walking across the street with my son or daughter and a dump truck broke loose, and there was only time to save one of you, I'm sorry, but you're dead meat. I'd save either of them before I'd save you. I care about you, I have some grasp of the value of your soul, but I don't love you like God loves you.

I guess you have to be a parent to understand what God did. He wanted to communicate the depth and breadth of his love, so he took that which was valued the most by him and exchanged it for us. He said, "I love you as much as my own kid. The proof is on this cross."

When a person understands what God did, there is only one appropriate response:

> *You ought to be so grateful that you would take your hands off your life and give yourself willingly and totally to the one who created you.*

Do you have to do that to be saved? No. Is some degree of commitment required to be born again? Yes. The heart has to change. Must you believe? Of course.

Jesus Christ wants you to become his bondslave. But to do so you have to make a major decision. *What do I do with my carp when God asks for them?*

COUNT IT ALL CARP

The apostle Paul was a tough guy. Not physically. He wasn't big and burly like Peter. But, he was certainly determined, and once a course was plotted, he was absolutely set in his ways. There wasn't a wishy-washy bone in his body. And driven. A classic Type A personality. But unlike typical hard-nosed fightin' Rocky types, the Apostle had quite a way with words. Paul wasn't mistaken for Hermes, (the god of oratory) for nothin'.[1] The man could talk, and his toughness occasionally came through in his speech.

Once, he was confronted with a proposition suggesting we ought to sin so God would have more opportunities to demonstrate his grace. Some translations state that Paul responded, "God forbid," "May it never be," "By no means," or other words to the same affect.[2] No way! Those are Christianized versions intended to avoid offense. In the process, the meaning and emotion were removed. I think *The Cotton Patch Gospels* says it the closest the English language comes for what Paul said in the Greek: Hell no!

He used the same technique in Philippians to communicate another concept.

> What is more, I consider everything a loss compared to the surpassing greatness of knowing Christ Jesus my Lord, for whose sake I have lost all things. I consider them *rubbish*, that I may gain Christ and be found in him, not having a righteousness of my own that comes from the law, but that which is through faith in Christ—the righteousness that comes from God and is by faith (Philippians 3:8-9 italics mine).

The NIV uses the term *rubbish*, but King Jimmy called it *dung*. Dung! In Luke 13:8 it meant manure, as in fertilizer. But in Philippians it meant "refuse to be thrown to the dogs." "I do count them but dung," Paul said with clarity.

His choice was a word of emphasis. Almost coarse, but not quite. However, everyone knew exactly what it meant: Anything that took you away from the bull's-eye was considered dung. It was a collective word, too. Conceptually, it rounded up everything extraneous, threw it into one pile, and gave it a label. The only English word that does the term justice is *crap*. As in Paul's case, it is not a substitute for the "S" word. But it is on the edge of coarseness and might be offensive to you. That's why I've called it *carp*.

Look back to the passage. "I consider everything a loss." "I have lost all things." "I consider them rubbish . . . dung . . . carp." That's the progression. In other words:

Anything in a life that interferes with growth in Jesus Christ is carp.

Anything that's more important to you than the Son of God is just foul fish.

Paul made it clear. Let go of it all 'cause it's all carp. It's a decision he made. A choice. He had a change of mind. It was an issue of faith.

Would you make the same choice?

Would you do the same with your past? It's just carp. Why not take everything you have, everything you will have, everything you are, and everything you ever will be and thrust it all into the hands of God? He knows what to give back, what to hold on to until you can handle it, and what to throw out.

Are you willing to give God whatever he asks for when he asks you for it? Maybe he'll just want a carp at a time. Perhaps he'll demand the whole school. I don't know how he'll do it with you but he'll never ask more of you than you are capable of handling. That's God's promise:

No temptation has seized you except what is common to man. And God is faithful; he will not let you be tempted beyond what you can bear. But when you are tempted, he will also provide a way out so that you can stand up under it (1 Corinthians 10:13).

What do you think? Did you say yes to becoming his bondslave? I hope so. But if you did, look out. After you make that decision he'll get you ready for service. That happens in his crucible called life.

IT'S HOT IN THE POT

When a person shuts his or her ear in the Lord's door and rejects freedom by becoming God's bondslave, the first stop is usually the pot. God begins to cook the impurities (carp) out of you, and like purifying precious metal, the dross of your life rises to the surface to be scraped off, leaving you a little more like Jesus. The process for those who are sold out is described in Zechariah 13:9:

"I will refine them like silver and test them like gold. They will call on my name and I will answer them; I will say,'They are my people,' and they will say, 'The LORD is our God.' "

The Levites served as priests. They represented God to the people and the people to God. Those who would be his ministers, whether in full-time service or making tents, should consider the consequences of Malachi 3:3:

"He will sit as a refiner and purifier of silver; he will purify the Levites and refine them like gold and silver. Then the LORD will have men who will bring offerings in righteousness."

Those who give themselves to the Lord will be refined and purified. He has to get rid of their carp. It's hot in the pot. I have to admit, it's not always fun. I don't know who it was who said, "God has not used anyone greatly who he has not hurt deeply." I don't find it to be a universal rule, but it is generally true. There are some sold-out servants who don't seem to have had crucible experiences, but most have spent some time in the pot.

And it hasn't been a one-time cooking for me either. Every now and then God continues the refining process and cuts away another part of my flesh. Lately he hasn't even used anesthetic. It's been hard. There has been some dross down deep that he hasn't demanded until recently.

But it's worth it.

The apostle Paul made the decision to be a bondslave. He gave everything to the Father and received contentment and the fruit of the Spirit: love, joy, peace, patience, kindness, goodness, faithfulness, gentleness and self-contol. As a result, Paul was able to survive the testing.

The Romans threatened to kill him. Remember what he said?

"Great. I'll be with Jesus."

"Okay, since that doesn't faze you, we'll torture you instead."

"Wonderful. I'll identify with the sufferings of Christ."

That doesn't bother him. "We're gonna throw you in jail and rotate the guard every four hours. Whaddaya think of that?"

"Marvy, I'll be able to lead two or three of them to Christ each day."

He doesn't mind that either. There was only one thing left to do: They released him!

What do you do with a guy who has nothing to lose? Anything. That's the point. Bondslaves are tied to Christ. Their eyes are on the eternal; they can't be devastated by anything in this life. They have given everything up for Christ.

Wow! What a way to be!

Becoming God's bondslave is what this book has been all about. I've done what I can to make you uncomfortable if you have been living in the fuzzy gray. Why take a chance on your salvation? The next move is yours.

WRAP UP

1. Become a bondslave.
2. Give up your carp each time God asks for one.
3. Getting fitted for service won't be easy, but it'll be worth it.

8

KICKING CARP

Mary and I sponsored the college department at our church for four years. One of the girls was wrestling with carp when we talked. "I want to party, drink, and mess around," she confided.

"Why don't you?" I asked.

Her pause was long and thoughtful. Finally she looked up, "Because the whole deal's real," she said with finality.

When she realized that Christianity was real, the temporal things of this world lost their importance. She knew she had to cut the carp out of her life as God asked for them. She had no other choice . . . and neither do you and I. We just lost our options. Folks, the whole deal *is* real. There is only one thing left to do: what's right.

Are you ready to sell out to Christ? I hope so. Everything you've read in this book has been designed to bring you to the place where you want to make him Lord of your life. Get ready to submit to God and resist the devil (James 4:7). Let's kick some carp.

The purpose of *Something's Fishy* is twofold: (1) to scare the heaven into you if you've come to the realization that you don't know Christ; (2) to convince you to sell out to Christ if you're a lukewarm Christian.

IT'S TIME TO PRAY

You'll need to be alone. Eliminate distractions— make sure the kids or friends won't be coming in to bother you. And take the phone off the hook. Really! DO it, because it will ring for sure. It's the enemy's way of doing things. This is a battle the devil doesn't want to lose.

Get comfortable. Your body's position doesn't matter to God. Pray the following prayer out loud. That may seem silly, but do it anyhow.

> *Heavenly Father, your character goes beyond our ability to understand, but gives us insight into your nature.*
>
> *You are the great and mighty God of glory, sovereignty, and power. The creator and preserver of all things. Thank you for your greatness.*
>
> *You are the absolutely self-existent, eternal, and unchangeable God who has no beginning or end. A personal, continuous God who is righteousness, holiness, love, and redemption. Thank you for personally loving me.*
>
> *You are God Almighty, the all-sufficient one who nourishes, supplies, satisfies, and provides. Help me to use your gifts to be pleasing in your sight.*
>
> *You are the one who confirms ownership, mastership, and lordship, who is faithful in provision and protection. The Lord who claims obedience and*

service. Master, I am your servant—I desire to be your bondslave.

You are the God who will provide—you see needs and will meet them. A God who manifests himself to his people, you know my needs and I trust you to meet them.

You are the God who heals—physically, emotionally, spiritually, and morally. The healer of sickness and sorrows. I have been beat up by life, and I need the kind of healing only you can provide. Please heal me.

You are the God who sanctifies—dedicates, consecrates, and sets apart as holy. Thank you for setting me apart as holy through Jesus Christ my Lord.

You are the God of peace—the restorer of man to peace with God through the atonement.

You are the God of righteousness—the God who as the Righteous One is the basis for our justification, acquittal, and acceptance. Thank you that in spite of my shortcomings, I can be a part of everlasting righteousness.

You are God my shepherd—the one who feeds and leads me. Companion, friend . . . you are tender, intimate, and personal. Thank you for your intimate care and love for me.

You are the God who is there—the one who never leaves me nor forsakes me. The one I can always turn to. Father, I turn to you now in the name of Jesus Christ.

> *Father, defeat the agencies of the devil for me right now. Be my banner insuring victory. Be the standard I can turn to as the battle begins, giving me confidence in the outcome.*

Now pray to God and verbally rebuke the enemy. Pronounce (out loud and with authority) the following:

> *In the authority of the risen Christ and in the power of the Resurrection, I come against all principalities and powers assigned to me by the enemy. I call them to the light of the judgment of the Holy One of Israel. I pronounce shattered all influences that are keeping me under satan's authority.*

> *Specifically, in Jesus' name I come against any agency of the enemy directed at holding back repentance or belief.*

RESPONSE TO A CHANGED HEART

Don't skim the words that follow. Make them a matter of deep reflection. The condition of your heart is crucial to effective praying.

A right heart, coupled with belief in Christ, makes a prayer out of words.

So, let's have a spiritual electrocardiogram. Psalm 139:23-24 is a great place to start. Don't just read it through. Pray.

> Search me, O God, and know my heart; test me and know my anxious thoughts. See if there is any offensive way in me, and lead me in the way everlasting.

Pray through the verses again to make sure you mean what they say. Don't try to snow God, you can't pull the wool over his eyes.

It's time for a repentance check. If you are ready to do an about face and return to the Lord by going his way, pray through the next two verses. Ask God if these verses apply to you:

> Let the wicked forsake his way and the evil man his thoughts. Let him turn to the LORD, and he will have mercy on him, and to our God, for he will freely pardon (Isaiah 55:7).
>
> Rend your heart and not your garments. Return to the LORD your God, for he is gracious and compassionate, slow to anger and abounding in love, and he relents from sending calamity (Joel 2:13).

Commitment is essential in lordship. It wasn't an option for Solomon. It's not an option for you or me either.

> "And you, my son Solomon, acknowledge the God of your father, and *serve him with wholehearted devotion* and with *a willing mind*, for the LORD searches every heart and understands every motive behind the thoughts. If you *seek him*, he will be found by you; but if you forsake him, he will reject you forever." (1 Chronicles 28:9)

The concepts to reconsider from the previous verse are "serving with wholehearted devotion," "serving with a willing mind," and "seeking him." Are they things you want to do? Are they desires that reflect your heart? Don't kid yourself if they aren't. That's a choice you should talk to God about before going on. Stop and pray about serving with wholehearted devotion, serving with a willing mind, and seeking him.

Finish your examination by praying through the following verses. Do they reflect your innermost desires?

Deuteronomy 6:5: Love the LORD your God with all your heart and with all your soul and with all your strength.

Psalm 119:2: Blessed are they who keep his statutes and seek him with all their heart.

Proverbs 3:5: Trust in the LORD with all your heart and lean not on your own understanding;

Jeremiah 29:13: You will seek me and find me when you seek me with all your heart.

Joel 2:12: 'Even now,' declares the LORD, 'return to me with all your heart, with fasting and weeping and mourning.'

If you were sincere in the evaluation of your heart, repentance is no longer an issue for you. And when you mess up, (notice I said *when*, not *if*) confess it and move on with your life. The apostle Paul is a great example of a repentant man who continued to sin—but he didn't want to. He sincerely wanted to live a life that was pleasing to God. He had a repentant heart. Do you?

Consider the prayer I prayed when I became God's bondslave at Hume Lake. Make it your own:

God, I don't fully understand everything that's going on right now, but I acknowledge that you made me, therefore you must know what's best

*for me—I don't. I want to take my hands off my
life and give you control. I don't know what that
will mean, but I don't want to run it anymore. I
don't want to say no to you anymore. I know I
will say it, but in my heart I don't want to. If you
can still use me, I'm yours.*

---

*Do you want to live a life that is pleasing to God?
If you do, you have a repentant heart.*

Perfection is impossible. But your desire for godliness
is the evidence of a changed heart.

WELCOME TO KICK CARP LAKE

Congratulations! Welcome to Kick Carp Lake . . .
Tweener's Bog is no place for Christians. You have made
a commitment to be sold out and the only way you can
put on trout's clothes is by messin' and not confessin'.
So, press on with your faith.

If you've read this far and still need one last nudge,
this is it. Like the blind beggar, you are standing on the
edge of the pool of Siloam. Let me tell you how he got
there.

In a church setting, I stand in front of the audience,
eyes closed, with my right hand up and extended, pre-
tending to have a cup in my hand. The dialogue goes
something like this:

I'm a beggar. Blind. Have been since birth. I've
never seen a shape, a color, or a man's face. Words like
billowy blue or *cloud* mean nothing to me. My senses cannot encounter them.

This is my spot. Right here outside the temple down
the steps from the entrance. It's a good place to do what
I do. Most everyone comes by.

I sit out here and beg for shekels. If I don't get a couple a day I can't survive. As it is, my clothes are tattered, dirty, and old. I sleep outside. It's especially difficult during the winter cold and the rains of spring. I can't bathe regularly. I have lice. Life is hard.

Every now and then a pompous Pharisee comes by with an entourage of people, toots a horn, and draws a crowd. Then he plays bombardier with a coin, dropping it from as high as he can to make as much noise as possible when it hits my cup. Everyone applauds his generosity as he struts away. Big deal! It's okay with me though. I need the shekels.

Hey! I hear a ruckus. Men shouting.

They're getting closer. I think they're coming by me! What did that guy say? He asked if I was blind because of my sin or my father's sin!

Humph! I probably won't get a shekel from him.

Wait a minute! His friend just stuck up for me and said sin had nothing to do with my blindness—it was so God could be glorified. His voice is great—so soothing. This guy likes me. Maybe I'll get a shekel.

Great, he's coming up toward me.

Boy is he close—in my space, if you know what I mean. He must be on his haunches. I'm afraid to stick my cup out too far. What if I punch him in the nose?

What was that? He spit. Right between my feet! The overspray is on my ankles. He's spitting again. He's not stopping!

Now he's making mud pies. Moosh-moosh.

I don't believe this guy! He said, "Here's mud in your eye" and smeared dirt and saliva over my eyes.

And here I sit. Stunned. Shocked.

Now this guy has the nerve to tell me to take a hike and get my sight. Can you believe it? He said, "Go to the Pool of Siloam, wash, and then you'll see."

What a long shot. This is a real flyer. A wild-goose chase for sure. How dumb does he think I am? He must think I'm one of those suckers born every minute that ol' P.T. Barnum talked about. What have I got to lose? Maybe he's for real. I think I'll go for it.

>● >● >●

The story of the blind beggar can be found in the ninth chapter of the Gospel of John. It reads better if you let your mind's eye wander to catch the flamboyancy of Christ. One thing is for sure, Jesus had to have done some serious spitting. Maybe even a lugy or two.

So, the beggar took off walking toward the Pool of Siloam. The trip wouldn't be without it's distractions. He'd never been there before. He was tempted to quit before he even got there. But he made it.

The rest of the story unfolds at the Pool of Siloam.

>● >● >●

Whew. I made it. Talk about tough. I thought I was a gonner when that donkey cart bumped me. And that camel! Was his breath something else or what? I'm all scraped up, but I'm okay. And it took most of the afternoon, but at least I'm finally here.

I'd like to jump in, but blind men don't jump.

Should I stick my toe in? Why not?

Man, the water's colder than I expected. Gives me goose bumps when it gets to you know where. Better take one more step and get it over with. I'll go in to my waist.

This is the dumbest thing I've ever done. Giving up my spot and my shekels. Dumb. No food today. Foolish. I don't even know the guy who sent me here. I'm such a sucker. And here I am up to my rear end in stagnant water with mud on my face, made from some smooth-talkin' dude's spit no less. Gullible. I really am. I'll bet he's having a great laugh at my expense right now. I'm a fool.

Oh, I hope it works. Here goes.

> ⋙

When the blind man came up, he could see. Shapes . . . color . . . depth . . . movement . . . size. Visual perception. Twenty/twenty. He had had so many mental images of what things would look like—all were being revised. Things are never the way we imagine them.

He was overcome with gratitude. So thankful was this man, so filled with elation, that he ran around town telling everyone what happened. He was sold out to the one who had given him his sight. He wouldn't recognize him when he saw him, but he decided to serve him when he found him.

Are you still at the side of the pool? Are you trying to decide whether to jump? Remember the frogs on a log? Give up your agenda, jump. Sell out and get blessed.

EPILOGUE

ANSWERING THE BIG QUESTION

I asked a big question in chapter one: Was I saved during that fifteen-year period between praying to receive Christ at fourteen and selling out at twenty-nine?

The answer is yes.

How do I know?

Even though I struggled with distractions in the world for a long time, I wanted to be right with God, and I believed Christ died for my sin. I never wavered in my belief, even though it took fifteen years for it to play out.

In my case, genuine faith was there, and with it salvation. I was a bass in trout's clothes. The presence of the Holy Spirit is proof. At twenty-nine I started listening to the Father, began killing my carp, and swam back into Kick Carp Lake again.

I am fully aware of the Spirit of God having worked in me over the years. I wanted salvation, believed, and repented. The Holy Spirit was there. I was lukewarm, but I was saved. I am sure now, but I wasn't sure then. That's the problem with livin' in Tweener's Bog. There is little assurance when you're swimmin' around in murky waters.

But, I've responded to the carp hunt. Although I've still got a few carp in my life, the Lord is producing fruit. I'm swimmin' in Kick Carp Lake.

Hey! We're finished and I'm outta here. You've either decided to cut the carp or you haven't. There isn't any more I can do.

FOOTHOLDS

If you have spent a lengthy part of your past in sin, there may be some footholds that need to be dealt before you can kick carp. Consider the following questions:

Do you have an unforgiving spirit? Are you harboring a root of bitterness toward another person, God, or yourself?

Is there any form of immorality in your life? Are you making subtle compromises in the area of your sexuality? Did you give your virginity away? Did you have sex with your mate prior to marriage?

Evaluate your goals in light of what God would want for you. How are your priorities? Have you been chasing after the things of this world?

Taking back the ground lost to sin can be an important step in getting the devil off your back. If you need some help in that area pick up a copy my book *Counterattack*. It also will provide a logical progression in your spiritual development. Your local Christian bookstore can get it for you. If, for some reason, they can't get it, write me.

If I am ever speaking in your area, come, greet me, and let me know what you decided about your carp. I need the encouragement. We'll shake hands, hug, laugh, cry, or something.

And by the way, I have a monthly newsletter called *Obedient Thoughts*. Write, and I'll put you on the mailing list:

Jay Carty
Yes Ministries
2850 S.W. DeArmond Dr.
Corvallis, OR 97333

I rarely ask for money, so you're pretty safe. You can go six to nine months without having any feelings of guilt at all. You'll know where I'm speaking because my schedule is always included. I'd appreciate your prayers, and I'd love to meet you.

If you need a speaker at your church or for your group, give me a shout (503-754-7547). I also have audio tapes. Let me know if you're interested.

May God richly bless you.

Be a kick-carp bass in Kick Carp Lake.

APPENDIX

NETTING A FEW THAT GOT AWAY

This chapter contains all the information I thought was important for you to know that my editor (being the hard-nosed person that she is!) wouldn't allow me to keep where I originally placed it. (She said something about interrupting the flow of the book. I said, "Who cares?" She said, "I do! Do you want this book published . . ." I said, "Don't play dirty with me!" Guess who won.)

I've chosen to use a question-and-answer format because I think that's the clearest way to address these issues. Not everything in this chapter will apply to every reader. Feel free to pick and choose those which interest you. (Aren't I generous?)

1. After reading this book, I realize that I'm not a Christian. How can I receive Christ and be assured of my salvation?

To receive Christ as Savior you must believe that Jesus Christ died for your sins. Read through the following verses and see what you think.

John 3:16 "For God so loved the world that he

gave his one and only Son, that whoever believes in him shall not perish but have eternal life."

John 3:18 "Whoever believes in him is not condemned, but whoever does not believe stands condemned already because he has not believed in the name of God's one and only Son."

John 3:36 "Whoever believes in the Son has eternal life, but whoever rejects the Son will not see life, for God's wrath remains on him."

John 6:40 "For my Father's will is that everyone who looks to the Son and believes in him shall have eternal life, and I will raise him up at the last day."

John 6:47 "I tell you the truth, he who believes has everlasting life."

John 8:24 "I told you that you would die in your sins; if you do not believe that I am the one I claim to be, you will indeed die in your sins."

John 11:25 Jesus said to her, "I am the resurrection and the life. He who believes in me will live, even though he dies."

1 John 5:13 I write these things to you who believe in the name of the Son of God so that you may know that you have eternal life.

What did you decide? Do you believe Jesus Christ died for your sin?

The Resurrection holds the key to the reality of the Christian faith. Either Jesus overcame death, or he was consumed by it. "If you confess with your mouth, 'Jesus is Lord,' and believe in your heart that God raised him from the dead, you will be saved" (Romans 10:9). If you don't believe Jesus conquered death, you can't expect him to conquer it for you. Did he really do it?

What do you think? No, that won't do. Thinking is not enough. What do you *believe?* Did he die for your sins? Did he come out of the grave alive?

Did you say YES? Then invite him in.

Jesus is calling out to you. "Here I am! I stand at the door and knock. If anyone hears my voice and opens the door, I will come in and eat with him, and he with me" (Revelation 3:20). All you have to do is turn the knob and open the door. He does the rest. He makes you a child of God—forgiven, and puts you in a right relationship with the Father.

Open the door and invite him in. Pray as follows:

Heavenly Father, I do believe that Jesus Christ died to save me from my sins. I do believe he conquered death for me. And within the framework of my limited spiritual understanding, I have a heart that is desirous of being pleasing to you. Having searched my life, I realize the futility of finding meaning without you.

Therefore, by faith I choose to open the door of my life to you, and I willingly, gratefully, and expectantly invite you to come in. Save me from my sins and begin to mold me into the person you want me to be.

My prayer is made in the name of the holy Son of God, Jesus Christ, in whom I place my faith. Amen.

2. I've committed some pretty terrible sins in the past. Are there any that Christ didn't die for?

Years ago I cheated on my income tax, and I took a

pack of gum from a store as a kid. I'm a thief. I'm a liar, too. I've told some. I've cheated on tests, both in high school and college. I'm a cheater. And I've had some real naughty thoughts. Although I've never murdered anyone, I've committed a lot of the things that should keep a person out of the kingdom. I still am doing a few. I struggle with pride, boasting, greed, gossip, complaining, selfish ambition, temper, and maybe a few others. How can I be in?

Because Jesus died for all sin—period. But he died only for those who will claim their forgiveness. I've claimed it. What about those who won't claim what Christ did for them? Lost!

3. I realize we must be born again, but does God require that we all come to him in the same way?

If a person is going to enter into a personal relationship with the living God, isn't it likely that the method of entry into that relationship is going to be highly personal, and therefore unique? That's why it's so dangerous to expect people to do exactly what we did, or wonder about them if they don't.

Christ rarely led any two people to himself in the same way. He did it with a touch, a word, and with spit. And his demands varied as well. Sometimes belief was required, at times a person had to repent and believe, and in some instances only repentance was mandated. He knew what part of the salvation equation each person was missing.

For example, belief wasn't even a topic of consideration with the rich young ruler. He came asking Jesus what he had to do to be saved. Jesus only asked for repentance. The yuppie had to do something. He had to demonstrate a willing heart by trashing everything that was more important to him than God. Jesus never even mentioned belief.

Few there are who come to Christ the same way. How can they? God doesn't require the same things from each person. How could he? He promises not to allow us to be tempted beyond that which we are able to endure (1 Corinthians 10:13). That means he works the purification of our behavior in the direction of becoming more and more like Christ according to what we can handle at the time. Each person's background is so diverse, and we carry so much baggage from our past. He dumps the whole load on some, but portions it out on others.

How much commitment? How much belief? How much of these components is necessary for salvation? What's the correct mixture? Only God knows. A person may only need a part of the salvation message, but we have to preach it all—we don't know what's missing. That's why both repentance and belief must be in our statement.

4. I passed the test in Chapter Five, but I don't know exactly when I became a Christian. A lot of people I know remember the time, place, and date . . . I don't. Should I be worried?

Not necessarily. People with a classic conversion experience have a time, date, and a place to attach to what they did. They walked an aisle, came forward at camp, prayed in front of a television, knelt beside the bed with a loved one, or pulled the car off to the side of the road and prayed with a voice on the radio. You may not specifically remember your time and date, but you do know you are born again. Around 25 percent of the born-again population appears to fall in that category.[1]

Let me tell you about my friend, Johnny. Johnny was in a Bible study with me for two years. His wife came to Christ, his two kids came to Christ, and after two years he came up to me one day and said, "Jay, it happened."

"What happened?"

"I'm a Christian."

"Great, when did it happen?"

"I don't know."

"Was it last week?"

"I don't know."

"Was it two weeks ago?"

"I don't know."

"Was it six months ago?"

"Jay, I don't know. All I know is that as I stand before you, Christ is in my life, my sins are forgiven, and I'm a child of God."

For people who come to Christ as a process rather than a one-time transaction, apparently the components of salvation (belief with a changed heart) come together at different times. My friend Johnny believed, but that didn't save him. He was born again sometime during the next two years when all the components of faith came together. When the heart changes within a person who believes, belief becomes faith. Jesus promises to come in and flood that person with himself. He fills you and cleanses your sins. That's what he did for Johnny.

5. I haven't always had assurance of my salvation. Why do I suddenly feel like I know that I know that I know?

The best way I know to answer this question is to make an analogy. I want you to take a little test. Look at the following letters and determine which one is missing:

O T T F F S S E N __ ?

It could be an O since that's the letter starting the sequence. Perhaps it's an N since there is a single letter O preceding a double T (the single E could be preceding a double N). It could be a D spelling out the word *end* and putting an end to the string of letters.

Those explanations are all logical, but wrong. The missing letter is a *T*.

At this point most people do not know why it is a *T*. Yes, they know that it is (because I told them), but they don't know why. If you do not yet know why, you probably aren't very excited about the letter *T*. But if you know, you can hardly wait to show these letters to your friends, because you are excited about the letter *T*.

It's the same with Jesus Christ. Most people in the United States have heard his name and are aware that Jesus claims to be the Son of God and the Savior of mankind.

His is the most frequently used name in our nation. You'll hear it in locker rooms, on golf courses, and in business meetings. People shout it when they're happy, mad, surprised, and excited. It's the only proper name that is a swear word. But like the *T*, only those who are intimately acquainted with him are excited. Knowing about Jesus doesn't excite. Knowing him is very exciting indeed.

Let me help you come into an intimate relationship with the letter *T*. Look at the letters and repeat the following words: one, two, three, four, five, six, seven, eight, nine, ten. Did you have an "Ah ha!" experience?

Not yet? Do it again. Look at the letters and repeat the numbers one through ten out loud.

Most people have it by now, but just in case you don't, what is the first letter of each word as you count from one to ten?

O	T	T	F	F	S	S	E	N	?
n	w	h	o	i	i	e	i	i	e
e	o	r	u	v	x	v	g	n	n
	e	r	e			e	h	e	
	e		e			n	t		

The missing letter is the first letter of the word "ten."

When you finally understood, you had a classic "Ah ha!" experience. You don't know what happened, but you do know something took place. It occurred when you received Christ.

6. What if I have doubts about my salvation?

Doubts regarding the assurance of your salvation can come from God. If your soul is owned by the devil, you can count on God not giving you peace with where you are unless you want to be away from God. If that's what you want, you're not apt to hear from him. But if God wants you saved, and you are seeking him, you can count on being restless until you make the right choices.

However, if you are God's child, you may still have doubts. Satan loves to remind us of old sins and foul-ups. Its part of his fiery-dart routine. That's why it's good to examine your life for evidence of fruit. How did you do with the test in Chapter five? If you did well and you know that deep down you want to please God, the Bible says you're saved. Let me suggest several reasons why you may still lack assurance.

You might have lingering anger and a problem with forgiveness. Do you have a root of bitterness toward another person or toward God? The Word makes it clear: We are to forgive as God, in Christ, has forgiven us. Those who refuse to forgive the singular offenses against them, or who refuse to forgive themselves for what they have done, have difficulty believing that God can forgive the totality of their sin.

Forgiveness toward others is possible to achieve. You don't have to feel like doing it, you don't have to trust the person who wronged you, and you don't have to forget the offense to do it. Having successfully dealt with the issue of forgiveness toward others, you'll probably then realize how forgiven you really are by God, and you will realize assurance.

Perhaps you are looking for some special feeling or experience to confirm your salvation. Perhaps you've asked Christ into your life, but you don't feel any different. You're not sure what you should have felt, but you don't feel anything. Maybe you're looking for some kind of confirmation from God that the whole deal is real.

Another cluster of strugglers are those who won't allow themselves to grasp the free gift called grace. These people are still trying to earn God's favor with good works.

Remember, good works are the byproduct of a legitimate faith—works don't create faith. God will work changes in you. Your choices to act in godly ways and do godly things will be evidence of that. If this is your problem, study the concept of grace, and separate it from works. As you do, God's free gift of unmerited favor will hit you and you'll realize how saved you really are.

7. Can I lose my salvation?

Some say yes and some say no. I don't think so, and I firmly believe it. But there are some pretty bright people on both sides who equally love the Lord and who are equally well studied in the Word. Most of them are smarter than I am. However, it is only an issue for those who are trying to see how bad they can be. It's a non-issue for those who want their lives to be pleasing to God—they don't have to be concerned, regardless of which position they take.

Could a person who received Jesus choose to reject him later? I don't believe so, however I don't know for sure. But ask this question: Who would want to? The argument applies to so few people. If it were possible to be given the absolutes to heaven or hell, who in their right mind would choose hell? And if they weren't in their right mind, they'd be crazy, so would God even allow them such a choice? See? It's a non-issue.

Can a Christian do the things Paul talked about and lose his or her salvation? Again, I don't think so. But did they have it in the first place? Who knows? The "goin' for it" believer will have increased time between stumbles and decreased time between stumbles and confession. But for someone who's lukewarm, it's a huge issue. If you're lukewarm and are asking this question for fire insurance, look out!

8. I've prayed to receive Christ and really desire to please him with my life. However, I'm a recovering alcoholic with occasional binges. What about people who have addictions or compulsions? Can we be assured of salvation?

Will you settle for a definite "I don't know." Not for sure anyhow . . . not individually.

The sins of the parents are visited on the children, for several generations (Exodus 34:7), and generations of dysfunctional behavior are the norm these days. Compulsions and addictions are a partial result. At the least, if your parents were compulsive/addictive, your past will produce a predisposition toward compulsive and addictive behavior.

The Bible says:

> The soul who sins is the one who will die. The son will not share the guilt of the father, nor will the father share the guilt of the son. The righteousness of the righteous man will be credited to him, and the wickedness of the wicked will be charged against him (Ezekiel 18:20).

In other words, I'm responsible for my choices.

How many times will the Lord forgive me if I slip?

Seventy times seven (Matthew 18:22), meaning beyond all reasonable number. But the key to forgiveness is a repentant heart. Is a chronic sinner repentant? Sometimes. Young boys and some men struggle with compulsive masturbation and the images that go along with it. Each time there is a fresh vow for abstinence. It's the same with the alcoholic. They are deeply sorry after each mess-up. Is being sorry the same as being repentant? It wasn't for Judas, but it might be for you.

Regardless of our past, sinful compulsions and addictions are the result of our choices. Do you think God takes our past into consideration? I would think so. So, can an addict receive Christ and still be an addict? Sure. But can he have the assurance of his salvation? Maybe. I doubt it. I don't know. Who knows?

9. I've heard that there is a debate going on in Christian circles regarding what it means to have saving faith. What's the deal? How am I, a lay person, to know what's right?

Theologians are in a heated debate about what it means to believe with saving faith. The two sides who are arguing the loudest are both scholarly, thorough, trustworthy, and sincere lovers of Jesus Christ—committed to him and the careful study of his Word. But both sides strongly believe the other to be wrong, and both agree that one has to be.

If the most knowledgeable spiritual leaders in the country can't agree on the basics of salvation, you're right—what are we to do? When there's a mist in the pulpit there will be a fog in the pew. What are those who haven't been to Bible school, like you and me, to think? What side should we take? Do we have to take sides?

The two camps—"belief only" and "lordship/salvation"—have been formed around "what is belief?"

Basically, the belief-only side says believing that Jesus Christ died for you solves the problem of your sin. Repentance is defined as a change of mind about who Christ is, not something you do. Anything beyond a change of mind is considered a "work" by the belief-only people, and that would violate grace.

The lordship/salvation side says the same thing about believing but goes further by saying that repentance will show up in a progressively changed life. Faith will be expressed in behavior or there was no faith in the first place. No change equals no salvation.

There are two major downside risks in the lordship/salvation position. The first is misinterpreting works and trying to become good enough to be acceptable in the eyes of God. Works must be seen as a by-product of salvation, not a means of obtaining it. But it's easy to get confused.

The other downside revolves around those who struggle with grace and their understanding of faith. These people struggle with stumbling and wonder if they are practicers of sin (remember, stumblers are saved and practicers are lost). If lordship/salvation is wrong, they may spend a portion of their life wondering if they are saved, needlessly worried.

But if the belief-only position is wrong, then there will be a lot of people going to hell who thought they were going to heaven, who were given assurance without Christ being evident in their lives. Since there are a lot more "believers" than there are "doers" of the Word, the belief-only position is an unacceptable risk.

If we are going to err, let's do so on the safe side. Make sure works are an outcome of lordship, not a way to earn salvation, and don't give tweeners the assurance of their salvation.

It seems to me it's possible to win this battle and lose the war. If you're a tweener, and you choose belief only so you don't have to get serious about your faith, you could end up in hell. A choice for lordship solves the problem for you, regardless of who's right.

I know what I believe, but I'm not sure who's right. My position is that both sides are correct, since God varies his demands and requirements of us individually, according to his sovereign will. But, since no one can really be sure what's necessary (only God knows), lordship/salvation is the safer choice because it embraces both belief and repentance.

The argument has been hot in theological circles. But it's a war that nobody comes to. The masses don't much care, because the masses are in Tweener's Bog. The argument is a bit like pole-vaulting over mouse manure. We're making a much bigger deal out of the conclusion than should be made.

I believe it is more important to *not* decide who's right and who's wrong. The Body of Christ will be better off if those who want to know how bad they can be and still get in the kingdom, or those who are asking how good they have to be to just barely get in, can be left hanging. If the conclusion is "we're not sure," then the majority of the lukewarm cannot have the assurance of their salvation. If that is the conclusion, then both sides can be right and the middle can't be sure. I think that's the way it ought to be. Only the tweeners won't know. But I say, let the apathetic wonder.

What about those who won't come to the war? What about those who don't really care? What about those at Tweener's Bog? What about Luke Warren Trout? Hmmmmmmmmmm! I wonder. They should be wondering too.

10. I've prayed to become a bondslave—I want to sell out to Jesus. How can I keep from putting on trout's clothes and keep the carp out of my life? I don't want to become lukewarm.

A dear friend, who had a one-man ministry after which I patterned Yes! Ministries, gave the best single piece of advice anyone has ever given me about how to stay carp-free. "Jay," he said, "don't take the first $5." He was telling me not to compromise a little, because a little almost always leads to a lot.

I was put to the test early in the ministry and have continued to be tested monthly thereafter. When I speak at churches, tape and books are usually sold. A certain amount of the proceeds are in the form of cash. Naturally the cash is untraceable.

What is there to keep me from pocketing the dollars? Absolutely nothing. No one would ever know. Not the IRS, not my board; no single person would ever know . . . except me—and God. And that's what my friend was warning me about. Because after the first time, it's just a matter of zeros—$5 becomes $50, $50 becomes $500, and so on. A few carp quickly become a school.

One month I was a little short of money. That's when pocketing the cash is real tempting. I put $64 from tape sales in my wallet and used it to get home without entering it into the books. Over $40 remained burning in my britches five days later. Was I actually going to compromise the ministry for $64? I couldn't stand it, took out my check book, made up the difference, and put that money back into the ministry. And no, I didn't claim a deduction for my check written to Yes! Ministries, because it wasn't a gift. I was paying back a debt.

Once I purchased a Walkman to listen to tapes on planes and in airports when I travel. It was a justifiable expense in my mind at the time, but it was a no-no for Jay. I tried to rationalize for two weeks before I wrote a check back to the ministry. I thank God for the loudness and persistence of his voice. He hasn't yet allowed me to keep the first $5.

There are lots of ways to take $5. I cheated on a test in college once. I had to get a 3.6 GPA to keep my graduate scholarship, and I caved in to the pressure. It's interesting, I got a C. The next quarter, in the second sequence of the class, I prepared properly, took the same professor's test and got an A on the final. The professor accused me of cheating because the paper was so different from the quarter before. I learned a valuable lesson—the hard way. That first dishonest act is the same as taking the first $5.

A sensuous conversation, a glance or touch with someone other than your spouse, is the first $5. Played out it leads to adultery. The first lie to stay out of trouble is the first $5. It's not long until lying becomes comfortable. The first pack of gum lifted from you local 7-11 is the first $5. Unchecked it leads to stealing items valued with more zeros—and jail.

We lived next to a Navy base for years. There's a military term that's interesting—"comshaw." It's what military surplus is called after someone has taken it. The practice was so common it was no longer considered stealing. It was comshaw.

It's that kind of thinking that makes the Iran/Contra arms scandal and Watergate okay at the time. It's comshaw when you do it, but it's stealing when you get caught; it's politics when you do it, but it's illegal when you're found out. In the light of day it's clearly wrong, but as a continued compromise it's just an extension of what you've grown used to doing as a way of life. The whole PTL situation was a result of the first $5 having been taken and not returned. After the first $5 it just became a matter of zeros—six of them, in fact.

Take a lesson. Don't take the first $5. Don't compromise. Ask the Spirit of God to make you more aware of those times when you are entertaining wrong thoughts.

And make a commitment to take your thoughts and emotions captive to the obedience of Christ (2 Corinthians 10:5). Such a decision will go a long way toward keeping your life free of carp.

ENDNOTES

Chapter 2

1. Titus 3:3
2. Romans 7:11
3. 1 Corinthians 6:9; Galatians 6:7
4. Galatians 6:7
5. Psalm 139
6. W. E. Vine, *An Expository Dictionary of New Testament Words* (Fleming H. Revell, Old Tappan, N.J., 1966), p. 169.
7. Genesis 19:4, 5
8. 2 Peter 2:7, 8

Chapter 3

1. Author unknown.
2. Proverbs 11:14
3. This is a concept from my book *Counterattack*. It refers to being double-minded when you pray.

Chapter 4

1. Luke 8:26-31
2. Matthew 9:9

Chapter 5

1. James 2:20
2. Psalm 51:11
3. 1 Corinthians 6:19
4. Ephesians 4:30
5. Galatians 5:22-23
6. Most commentators agree that "these things" refers to the book of 1 John. Hodges and others hold a position that this term references the preceding paragraph, not the entire book. Although he has been well published and outspoken, his position remains a minority opinion.
7. 1 John 2:12-14, 24, 4:14, 16-19, 5:1-4.
8. 1 John 2:24, 28, 4:15, 5:5, 20
9. 1 John 3:3, 5:9-13
10. 1 John: 2:15-17
11. 1 John 2:3-6, 9-11, 3:11-20, 4:7-12, 20-21, 5:6-8
12. 1 John 2:20, 27, 3:21, 24, 4:13

Chapter 6

1. John 14:6
2. Numbers 21:5-9
3. Revelation 3:20
4. Philippians 2:12

Chapter 7

1. Acts 14:12
2. Romans 6:1

Appendix

1. For the last eight years I've preached in church settings and given a "Born Again" survey. This figure is from the data I collected.